O.M. Ungers: Works in Progress

Preface by Kenneth Frampton

Introduction by Gerardo Brown-Manrique

Published by the Institute for Architecture and Urban Studies and Rizzoli International Publications, Inc.

Catalogue 6

Contents

Kenneth Frampton
Preface 1

G. Brown-Manrique
Morphologies 7

Interview 20

Hotel Berlin 24

Architecture Museum 34

Schillerstrasse 42

Bremerhaven 52

Karlsruhe 62

Lutzowplatz 72

Braunschweig 80

Hildesheim 86

Konstantinplatz 94

Bibliography 104

Editors
Kenneth Frampton
Silvia Kolbowski

Managing Editors
Laura Bell
Silvia Kolbowski

Designer
Massimo Vignelli

Design Coordinator
Abigail Sturges

Copy Editor
Dorick Byard

Production
Madison Spencer

IAUS Exhibition Catalogues Program Co-Directors
Kenneth Frampton
Silvia Kolbowski

Trustees of the Institute for Architecture and Urban Studies
Armand Bartos, Chairman
Charles Gwathmey, President
Douglas H. Banker
Richard F. Barter
A. Bruce Brackenridge
Colin G. Campbell
Walter Chatham
Peter D. Eisenman
Ulrich Franzen
Frank O. Gehry
Gerald D. Hines
Eli Jacobs
Philip Johnson
Edward J. Logue
Gerald M. McCue
Robert M. Meltzer
Paul Rudolph
Carl E. Schorske
Frederieke S. Taylor
Marietta Tree
Massimo Vignelli
John F. White
Peter Wolf

Associate Director, Hamid Nouri

Fellows of the Institute for Architecture and Urban Studies
Diana Agrest
Deborah Berke
Julia Bloomfield
Peter D. Eisenman
William Ellis
Kenneth Frampton
Suzanne Frank
Mario Gandelsonas
Silvia Kolbowski
Rosalind Krauss
Lawrence Kutnicki
Joan Ockman
Stephen Potters
Robert Silman
Carla Skodinski
Anthony Vidler
Peter Wolf, Chairman

First published in the United States of America in 1981 by Rizzoli International Publications, Inc. 712 Fifth Avenue, New York, N.Y. 10019

©The Institute for Architecture and Urban Studies
8 West 40th Street
New York, N.Y. 10018

All rights reserved. No part of this book may be reproduced in any manner whatsoever without permission in writing from Rizzoli International Publications, Inc.
Library of Congress Catalogue Card Number 81-51438
ISBN 0-8478-0378-3

Typesetting by Myrel Chernick
Printed by Morgan Press, Inc.

The translations of the project descriptions were originally prepared by Bettina Brand, Leo Krumpholz, Alice Kuzniar, Jane Newman and John Smith.

O.M. Ungers and the Architecture of Coincidence

Kenneth Frampton

Oswald Mathias Ungers is one of the most distinguished and didactic architects of his generation. Old enough to have seen military service at the end of the Third Reich and young enough to have had the energy and the integrity to struggle against the spiritual and moral devastations of the aftermath, Ungers had already established his initial career by the late fifties, building extensively in Cologne and creating an international reputation for himself as a third generation modernist. From an urban point of view, his early work was already "contextual," while in stylistic terms it seems to have been situated between the British New Brutalist movement which Ungers admired, and the more deeply "textured" expression of Fritz Schumacher's *neue Backsteinbauen*[1] of 1917, which played such a seminal role in the early German movement. Thus, despite syntactical similarities—the common use of exposed concrete slabs and extensive areas of load-bearing brickwork—Ungers's expression remained distinct from the New Brutalist *briques apparentes* manner, since it was not only removed from Corbusian concepts of spatial order but also antithetical to the tradition of the freely manipulated mass so prevalent in Anglo-Saxon culture. Thus, in the Nippes housing scheme completed in Mauenheimer Strasse, Cologne in 1957, the morphological manipulations are rigorously grounded in a systematic, geometrical permutation, which counterchanges throughout the length of the typical terrace and is close, in its generative form, to parallel developments in the work of the Swiss architects, Ernst Gisel and Andre Studer, and to the Morrocan housing realized by Vladimir Bodiansky's *ATBAT Afrique* in the early fifties.

Ungers's acceptance of a chair at the *Technische Universität (TU)* in Berlin in 1963, not only brought about an abrupt close to this fertile building period, but also turned his attention unexpectedly toward the East and toward the long tradition of political and cultural exchange between Germany and the Soviet Union; a fertile exchange established intermittently across the traumas of revolution and reaction. Above all, Ungers became pedagogically involved with the heritage of Russian Constructivism, in all its formal and functional complexity. Thus, the megastructural urban interventions designed by his prime students during the period of his Berlin tenure seem to fuse two fundamentally antithetical traditions: on the one hand, the Russian avant-gardist thrust toward monumental and dynamic structural form; on the other, a fragmentary Piranesian poetic, appropriate to the devastated landscape of Berlin. It is important to note that these modest but densely articulated projects appeared in an avant-garde climate which as far as Berlin was concerned had been seemingly preempted by the various master plan proposals submitted for the Haupstadt Berlin competition of 1958, including organic, somewhat megalomaniacal schemes by Hans Scharoun and the partnership of Alison and Peter Smithson.

The shock of the European student revolt of 1967-1968, colored above all by the charismatic Rudi Dutschke and *les évènements de Mai,* coincided with the end of Ungers's tenure in Berlin and his subsequent move to America and to Cornell University; a move which added a further twist to what was already becoming an Odyssean saga of continually displaced experience. At Cornell, he reverted unpredictably to his original technocratic formation at the Technische Hochschule in Karlsruhe, where he had studied under Egon Eiermann, and he began to involve himself in projects which were oriented toward the modular rationalization of housing design and the cybernetic control of regional planning. The reductive precision of this work was not well received in the American liberal climate, either by those who subscribed to the Neo-Sittesque, *Collage City* position which was then prevalent at Cornell, or by the typical New York State bureaucrat, whose perennial pragmatism was hardly able to comprehend, let alone utilize, a mapping system of such global and abstract dimensions.

Ungers's nostalgia for Germany finally motivated his founding of the German-American Berlin Summer Academy, first held at the Kunstlerhaus Bethanien in Berlin-Kreuzberg in 1976. This reimmersion in the mnemonic panorama of Berlin caused Ungers to reevaluate his mega-Piranesian manner, which had been developed with Jurgen Savade in the mid-sixties in a series of projects including the Enschede student housing project (1964), the Tiergarten Museum (1964) and the German Embassy in Rome (1965). That this return was much more than a simple reversion to an earlier format is borne out by three projects made, without Savade, in the late seventies: the Hotel Berlin (1977), the Friedrichstadt Development (1977), and the Berlin Law Courts competition (1978). In each instance, the perimeter suddenly emerges in Ungers's work as a place-making paradigm against which the inevitable chaos of urban fragmentation may play its *coincidental* role.

In 1976, in a key essay entitled "Planning Criteria," Ungers established the essential position of his subsequent career, a stance which has since shaped, in a fundamental way, most of the projects illustrated in this catalogue. Among the principles that comprise this complex position, in part formulated as theory, in part as practice, two broad concepts appear to take precedence. On the one hand, priority is accorded to the heterotopic reality of the modern city, to its manifest status as a disjunctive panorama, fragmented by the incursions of life, time, development, and war. On the other hand, the policy is that of confronting this otherwise intractable morass with the concept of a boundary or frame, as this is, of necessity, embodied in the paradigm of the perimeter block. This confrontation between the place-form and the open city has led Ungers to address repeatedly the central problem of his method: that is, how to apply the device of the bounded domain without falling into the acritical rigidity of making both an untenable closure and an idealistic exclusion. This doubly articulated goal of achieving a dialectic between place-form and place-lessness was declared by Ungers five years ago when he wrote:

"The first criterion of my design is the dialectical process with a reality as found....The design is determined by the specific building task, by the integration into an existing context and also by the intensification of place. The architectural concepts are based upon the reinforcement of the *genius loci* out of which they grow and of which they are a part. What I want to show through the projects one could briefly characterize as an architecture as found or as some people call it, contextualism. It is also the rationalization of an existing reality. The second criterion which all the designs have in common has to do with the problem of planning and accident in several ways. First that accidents are sometimes turned into planning intentions or to put it in better terms, into an architectural event. Secondly, that the plan has at least two levels of definition, a primary and a secondary. The primary level determines the framework or the basic structure which organizes the space for a secondary event, which can be more accidental, spontaneous and if necessary, temporary."[2]

The relevance and fertility of this approach stems from the fact that the modern city is, by its very nature, both open and incomplete and that any attempt to reconstruct the *totality* of its former or mythical fabric is a deception. Such attempts not only contradict our present productive capacity, but also invoke the idealistic myth of the lost whole; a chimeric illusion which, aside from being instrumentally untenable, tends toward the kitsch policy of recapitulating the historic city in the form of an empty scenography.

This advocacy of selectively deconstructing metropoli was first fully elaborated in Ungers's 1977 project for Berlin, which he entitled, The City in the City. This policy planning thesis was based on the premise that Berlin, like most other modern capitals, has continually lost population over the past twenty years at the annual rate of one per cent. According to Ungers, the remedy for this demoralizing and physically debilitating exodus is to maintain and develop certain quarters as "islands" (*stadtinselen)*, thereby allowing for the gradual abandonment of the superfluous fabric, prior to its progressive replacement by green space. This strategy implies the poetic complement of the Neo-Romantic "city of memory," as opposed to that which Ungers calls the city of the unconscious. In specific terms what Ungers has in mind is something akin to the *Havellandschaft* as this was once envisaged by Friedrich Wilhelm IV in the form of a Romantic parkscape representing the whole of Humanist history. Ungers's Berlin proposal envisages a comparable formation, comprising semi-isolated urban sectors linked by a necklace of green archipelagos. One of the corollaries of this proposal was the idea of the *urban villa* which, based on the typical Berlin villa of the *Gründerzeit*,[3] was reinterpreted by the students of the Berlin Summer Academy as a freestanding, low-rise, multifamily housing typology (c.f. Ungers's 1975 proposal for Berlin-Lichterfelde).

Ungers's subsequent architectural work seems to reflect

this general urban strategy, whereby each building or aggregation is projected into its urban context as though it were a *semi-autonomous* addition to the street fabric. So that while Ungers's Lützowplatz proposal (1980) attempts to reconstitute something of the original urban form, it does so in such a way as to presume the minimum about any subsequent development of the surrounding infrastructure. Much the same could be claimed both for the Hotel Berlin (1976), where the entire building is conceived of as a perimeter block, that is, as a paradigmatic city in miniature, and the Ackerhof development designed for Braunschweig (1980) where clearly the attempt was to respond to the historic accretion of the city over time. Thus, an effort was made to mediate between the surviving medieval labyrinth to the East of the principal urban block and the arbitrary, faceted geometry of the *Wirtschaftwunder* department store which flanked the site at the western end.

The Ackerhof project also demonstrates Ungers's double-sided approach to the concept of typology, for, as is evident from his work to date, his attitude toward type varies according to the circumstances. Thus, where a given urban or architectural context still manifests a culturally valid typology, Ungers will invariably predicate the new work on the structure of the pre-existing urban pattern. However, when the context presents itself as a homogeneity that is too remote to be reinterpreted without degenerating into kitsch or alternatively has a heterogeneity that is too chaotic to be reintegrated, as in the case of Braunschweig, then the preferred stragegy is to reduce the type or its typical site, depending on circumstances, to a gridded matrix on which a series of ludic permutations are endlessly unfolded as in the case of Marburg (1976). These "exercises in style" seem to affirm the dissolution of cultural conventions and assert instead the free play of indifferent form.[4]

The Ackerhof project for Braunschweig exemplifies both of these approaches, for while a terrace housing typology sympathetic to the context was employed as a mediation between the Georg-Eckert-Strasse highway and the extant medieval fabric surrounding the Magnikirche, the adjacent block, bounded by the same highway and by the Olschlagen, was perceptively judged as being too diffuse for any kind of normative pattern. Hence it was exploited as a domain in which to play with arbitrary, modular elements including permutations on the urban villa and somehwat unconvincing parodies of other traditional residential forms.

This fugal attitude towards type is posited by Ungers as a criticism of the ideology of the perfect plan, although this heteroclitic approach to urban structure and typology yields at times dichotomous results which seem to be uneasily suspended between Romantic, conciliatory Piranesian aggregations and the abrasive iteration of geometrically controlled but nonetheless arbitrary type-forms. Certainly, this subversive approach to architectural form may be taken as a commentary on the absurdity of much of our *laissez-faire* development.

In his major public projects Ungers employs elements whose references are more specific, as in the projected Baden State Library in Karlsruhe, where the perimeter configuration, with its continuous inner arcades, makes multiple allusions to various works by Friedrich Weinbrenner, including St. Stephan's Church built on the adjacent block and the bath house he designed for Ettlinger Tor. Apart from certain similarities in plan formation, specific allusions abound throughout the form of the Library, above all in its layered and gabled roof structure which analogically alludes the Weinbrenner's ballroom design and his portico scheme for the Karlsruhe Marktplatz. On the other hand the intersecting open-web trusses of the main reading room clearly transcend the confines of local culture and allude in general terms to nineteenth-century institutional typology.

In some instances the entire work, rather than the structure alone, seems to find its precedent in nineteenth-century building, as in the Carlsburg Hochschule designed for Bremerhaven (1979) where the *parti* amounts to a nineteenth-century hybrid, predicated in part on the galleria and in part on the light court of the typical department store. The Carlsburg Hochschule is remarkable on two other counts: first, for its ingenious adaptation of the galleria form to the illumination and ventilation of the main laboratory space, flanked by perimeter offices, and second, for its allusion to the nineteenth-century *Rathaus*, in as much as the main floor is raised above grade with parking beneath. Such typological adaptations and allusions have no obvious limit with regard to their actual use. Thus, in the Hildesheim project (1980), the traditional covered market structure or urban loggia is left open to reinterpretation as either an exhibition hall, a theatre or a restaurant, while the Hotel Berlin is institutionally fixed by virtue of its being predicated on the precedent of the American grand hotel, despite its elemental articulation into wall, towers, glasshouse, and rotunda.

In the proposed refurbishing of the Constantine Square in Trier, the level of typological allusion is determined by the archaeological status of the site, where the decisive move has been to recommend the excavation of the original Roman street in order to reauthenticate the epoch of the monument. Apart from revealing the original plaza, this proposal is confined to a redefinition of the existing square through the provision of low and essentially ahistorical, pitched roof structures executed in precision masonry.

The German Architecture Museum in Frankfurt (1978) condenses much of Ungers's methodology in a single building. As an initial response to the task of converting an existing nineteenth-century double-villa, the architect opted for the strategy of providing a specific boundary not only in order to augment the capacity of the house, but also to transform, with a simple, symbolic gesture, a pre-existing residential structure into a public institution. At the same time, the erection of a story high wall around the entire site was intended to transform the house into an exhibit-in-itself.

Once again we are confronted with a scheme which is predicated on the theme of a "house within a house" wherein one membrane of the structure is used to encase another and so on. Thus the initial wall, together with a peripheral arcade encloses both the house and the garden while the roofed garden is centered about a light court or patio which is rendered as an open gridded cube enclosing an existing chestnut tree. In a similar way, the shell of the house envelops, first the peripheral circulation in the form of stairways, then an eight by twelve module reinforced concrete frame, rising for six floors, which in turn encloses a double cube light court built of steel and glass and structured about a grid measuring four by four by eight modules. The light court of the garden is open to the air and serves to light the surrounding galleries while the light court of the house is roofed over and helps to illuminate the exhibition rooms of the villa. Something close to Nikolaus von Kues's ontology of number[5] seems to be evoked here, in which a given syntax and proportion is to be taken as alluding to specific attributes. Thus, where the open cube in the garden may be assimilated to "nature," the closed double cube within the house is to be associated with "art."

The result seems to resonate with primal oppositions: nature versus art, garden versus house, horizontal versus vertical, concrete versus steel, old versus new, masonry versus frame, open versus closed, etc; or alternatively it may be read as a series of structural containers, moving from the perimeter towards the center, which oscillate between the poles of heavy, light, heavy, void, heavy, light, void. In this generic alternation which recedes toward a void, one is returned to the apotropaic, if not to say the alchemical attributes of the aboriginal house, to the mystical definition of a God as "a sphere whose center is everywhere and whose circumference is nowhere,"[6] and to the primeval temple where presence is embodied in the absence apparent at the center. There is at the same time a more specific reference to the Humanist villa; above all to the "room with four columns" at the core of Andrea Palladio's Villa Pisani of 1552, as is evident in the four central columns which, arranged in a square on the two lower levels, denote the plan of the light court above. The play here across time is apposite since the typical Palladian four-columned hall was initially conceived of as a covered porch or loggia. The other primary Palladian allusion is the stairs which, set to either side of the inner house, afford a discrete if not entirely concealed means of access to the principal floors.

Finally, this complex is open to a Semperian interpretation since the one obsessive element which permeates the entire work is the open structural frame. Here, as in Gottfried Semper's theory, the frame, together with the knot asserts itself as the aboriginal form of architectural construction. And here, with the exception of the hearth (which once again is an "absent presence"), Semper's "Four Elements of Architecture" may be readily identified as first the earthwork (the garden), second the wall and third the frame together with the roof. And it is this last—the quintessential skeleton and filigree vault—which will prove to be Ungers's most challenging task to date, when he moves to build these elements at a megastructural scale, as in his current proposed extension for the Frankfurt Fair site, the famous Frankfurt Messehalle, the first stage of which is now under construction.

In this extension of the exhibition volume, where so much of the accommodation is, of necessity, both neutral and modular, the typological references become surprisingly specific and complex. On the one hand, there is an allusion to one of the lesser known nineteenth-century megastructures, the Galleria Umberto 1 in Naples, whose structure is consciously echoed in the barrel and cross-vaulted steel arcade linking the old and new exhibition halls and connecting to multistory parking structures at its extremities; on the other hand, there are perimeter service walls, faced in masonry, and an equally massive system of tiered car ramps giving access to the parking on the top of the new hall. These last two introduce heavier, less "progressive" references; they promise a prospect of the Frankfurt Fair as an oneiric parkscape of Roman proportions with cypress studded bastions and ramps evoking Palestrina or the Villa Borghese or even Sans Souci. But the implicit reference or at least the most local is the allusion to the very origins of the modern fair, namely to Friedrich von Tiersch's *Festhalle* of 1907, whose pioneering Verendeel ribbed structure in welded steel is surely recalled in the gusseted and intersecting arcs of Ungers's *passagen*.

Notes
1. See Fritz Schumacher, *Das wesen des neuzeitlichen Backsteinbaus* (Munich, 1920). This was Schumacher's seminal reinterpretation of the German brick tradition, particularly as this applied to the Hamburg region. Schumacher was *Oberdaudirector* for Hamburg from 1919 to 1923, until he moved to Cologne to become deputy town councilor in charge of urban expansion.
2. See O.M. Ungers, "Planning Criteria," in *Lotus*, No.11 (Milan, 1976), p.13.
3. *Gründerzeit* refers to the founding period of the Imperialist Prussian State under Bismarck and above all, in the term *Gründerjahre*, to the years of reckless financial speculation that followed the Franco-Prussian War, 1871-1874.
4. In his book, *Theory and History of Architecture* (English translation, 1980), Manfredo Tafuri refers to the architecture of the "indifferent object" (Chapter 2). See also his essay "L'Architecture dans le boudoir" published in *Oppositions*, No.3 (May, 1974).
5. From time to time in his theoretical work, Ungers refers to the writings of the mid-fifteenth-century German philosopher, Nikolaus von Kues (1401-1464), otherwise known as Nicholas de Cusa or Nicolas Cusanus. Above all Ungers refers to the *Coincidentum Oppositorum* in which von Kues develops the notion of the "convergence of opposites," which Ungers construes as an early philosophical intimation of his method.
6. See Jasper Hopkins, *A Concise Indroduction to the Philosophy of Nicholas de Cusa*, (University of Minnesota Press, 1978, second edition). On p.13 Hopkins writes of von Kues's assertions that "God is a sphere whose center is everywhere and whose circumference is nowhere. This statement...is not original with Nicholas but derives from Pseudo-Hermes Trismegistrus's *Book of Twenty-Four Philosophers*, a compilation of the late twelfth or the early thirteenth century."

1 T.H. Twente, Enschede, Netherlands, 1964. O.M. Ungers. Site plan and axonometric.

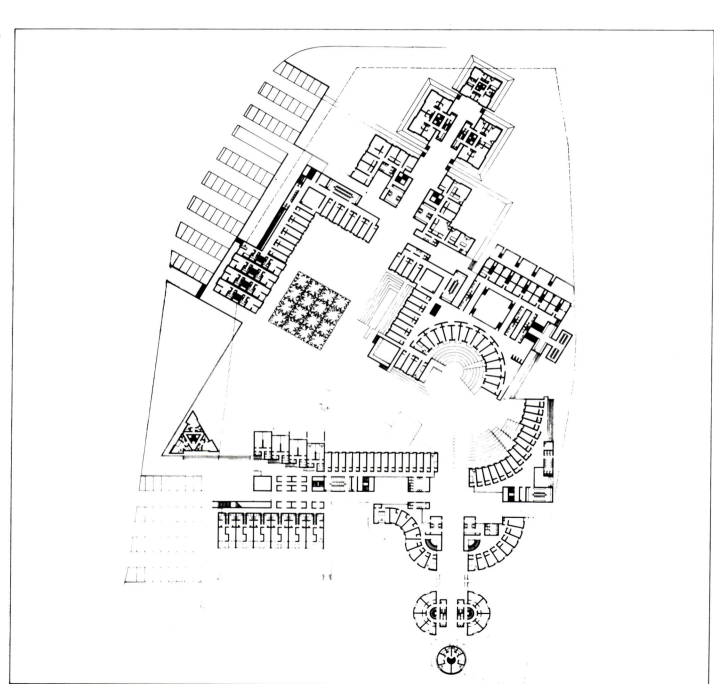

Morphologies, Transformations and Other Stories: Recent Work by O.M. Ungers

Gerardo Brown-Manrique

With cities, it is as with dreams: everything imaginable can be dreamed...cities, like dreams, are made of desires and fears...
Italo Calvino, *Invisible Cities*

Since 1950, O. Mathias Ungers has had an extensive career as an architect in Germany and America. During this time he has built over thirty structures, he has been widely published, and most importantly, his many proposals have had a significant impact on the development of contemporary architecture, particularly during the last fifteen years. Much of his earlier work has been of interest because of the manner in which it diverged from the norm in postwar German architecture. However, it is the work that Ungers has produced since 1965 that has brought him considerable international acclaim.

This work is the result of a design approach that by its very nature responds to specific programmatic requirements through the investigation of diverse sets of conditions. It has always reflected the context and structure of the city, its history and evolution. Ungers's design process explores all possible variations, all alternative answers to the problems which each program poses, instead of proposing a singular response derived from a narrow set of concerns. Ungers writes that he views "...the design process as a statement in transformation from one stage to another...never in its... final product," and that "we always see design in alternatives, which means their transformation, which means their morphology."[1]

One can generalize that this design approach identifies these alternatives based on diverse and often divergent sets of criteria, involving the investigation of structural and historical developments in the city and of specific building types identified *a priori*. This process results in proposals that in some manner reflect the local conditions and traditions. In an essay entitled "Towards A New Architecture" (1960), Ungers and Reinhard Gieselmann state:
"What architecture desires is the perfect expression of content, [since] architecture is a vital penetration of a multilayered, mysterious, evolved reality, its creative function is to manifest the task by which it is confronted, to integrate itself into that which already exists, to introduce points of emphasis and rise above its surroundings. Again and again it demands recognition of the *genius loci* out of which it grows."[2]

In some cases this investigation can be characterized by the identification and transformation of specific abstract elements. Particular geometries, variations in articulation of both plan and envelope, the combination of various volumetric variables—all these can be equally present, but of greater importance are those qualitative characteristics found in specific models or archetypes which can only be determined through a creative, intuitive investigation. In this regard Vittorio Gregotti writes:
"...starting from these fixed points [in historic and geographic space]...[Ungers] weaves a web of answers, a rigid range of syntactical alternatives which seem to be aimed at exhausting all the permutations of a linguistic typology of architectural solutions... [which] in Ungers's scheme of things, stress above all the concept of place, both spatial and historical."[3]

Ungers specifies the possible elements of this web including "...images, metaphors, models, analogies, symbols and allegories" which, used as design elements, form part of what Ungers believes is "...nothing more than a transition from purely pragmatic approaches to a more creative mode of thinking. It means a process of thinking in qualitative values rather than quantitative data, a process that is based on synthesis rather than analysis."[4]

One finds such an approach in the 1964 proposal for student housing at the T.H. Twente in Enschede, the Netherlands, (fig. 1) where Ungers initially investigated all the possible variations and combinations of elements derived from three distinct geometries—the circle, the square, and the triangle. These variants are then combined into specific elements so that the proposal embodies these elements as the constituents of a city:
"The plan reassembles a quasi-miniaturized city with components and elements recollected from actual city plans. One discovers all the prototypical parts and set-pieces, the basics of the larger counterpart: the individual house, the urban block, the building complex, the object in the garden,

the street and the plaza, the individual environment as well as the collective one. Private and public functions complement each other in an environment composed of citations embracing a morphological continuum of housing forms and residential types."[5]

In other cases the proposal derives from specific characteristics to be found adjacent to the site, as in the Grünzug-Süd redevelopment proposal for Cologne-Zollstock (1963-1966) (fig. 2). Despite their appearances, these projects have not simply evolved out of straightforward investigations. For instance, while one can argue that the Berlin-4th Ring proposal (1972) and the Roosevelt Island project, New York (1975) deal with the idea of abstract typologies and with a particular response to the contextual conditions of the site, one cannot conclude that these and subsequent projects are nothing more than abstract responses to a given context.

As a further example, the design for the new addition to the Schloss Morsbroich Museum in Leverkusen (1976-1980) involves the identification of specific elements at various levels. The design results not only from the transformation of the building type found on the site (the semi-circular ancillary buildings that surround the castle), but also from the purposeful attempt to explore the evolution of the building type in a more comprehensive sense, that is, an evolution comparable to the transformation of Abbe Laugier's "Primitive Hut" in the history of classical architecture. Ungers's own work manifests such transformations, as, for example, that from space defined by greenery to an enclosed space defined by stone.[6] Similarly, the proposal for the new courthouse complex and Turkish consulate in Berlin (1979) makes a commentary on the structure of the city along its boundary with the Tiergarten and at the same time reflects the typology of the courthouse.[7]

It is important to discuss these parallel tracks, this web of approaches that Ungers traverses in order to understand that he is not simply working with historical allusion, as is the current fashion in some circles. A thorough understanding of the city and its history in the light of how one might reapply its lessons is what Ungers seeks in his proposals. The proposal for the new Museums of Prussian Culture in Berlin (1964) (fig. 3) comprises another such investigation. Once more Ungers proposes a commentary on the city, only in this case not the city as it exists in the abstract, but rather as it is in fact, as was the case in his Enschede project. Instead he addresses both Berlin as it once was, complete with its historical cultural center, the Museumsinsel, and Berlin as it now exists, with its isolated western sector (fig. 5). The Museums project is conceived of as a complex of buildings, each housing specific museums, and all organized about a major public arcade. The uniqueness of each element reflects its individual functional requirements, but more importantly, "...the design of the different museum blocks reflects the historical spectrum, reaching from an almost rural courtyard building to the design of a block within the block and the most refined interior. The museum complex reassembles historical antecedents, memories and events of the city or of places related to the objects to be exhibited."[8]

Marco Polo describes a bridge, stone by stone.
'But which is the stone that supports the bridge?'
'The bridge is not supported by one stone or another,' Marco answers, 'but by the line of the arch that they form.'
Kublai Khan remains silent, reflecting. Then he adds: 'Why do you speak to me of stones? It is only the arch that matters to me.'
Polo answers: 'Without stones there is no arch.'[9]

Ungers does not simply seek a basis for design in the existing urban structure. The process of designing through morphological transformations requires that new types be introduced, that new relationships, definitions, and concepts of space be created which will in fact form part of the typological continuum. In Ungers's hands, there is a constant rethinking and restructuring of the process. His more recent proposals have become more involved with the use of building typologies and historical antecedents. Among these, the projects for the Schlossplatz/Museumspark in Braunschweig (1976) (fig. 4), the Hotel Berlin (1977), and the new Badische Landesbibliothek in Karksruhe (1979-1981) (fig. 6) involve, at varying scales, the identification and *transformation* of these antecedents. In its evolving form, Ungers's design approach becomes more of a pro-

2 *Grünzug-Süd Redevelopment, Cologne-Zollstock, 1962-1966. O.M. Ungers. Site plan.*

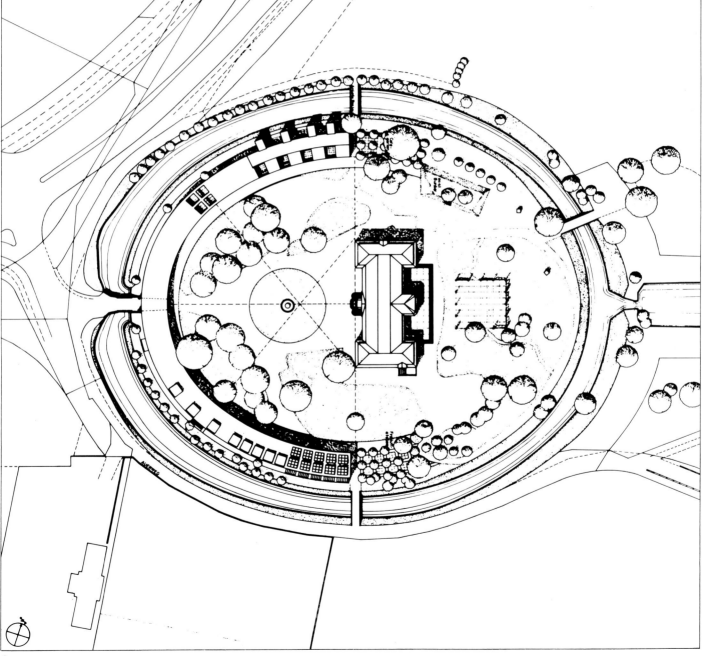

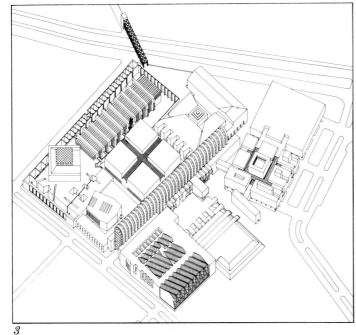

3

cess which requires the understanding of fundamental historical conditions rather than one which only interprets the existing elements. Thus, the urban analysis of Braunschweig and the subsequent proposals for the urban parks concentrate first on the synthesis of the essence of the city through a historical and morphological analysis of the identifiable parts of its structure—for example, the existence of an area formed by a regular grid or one that is radial in nature. These phenomena are analyzed first in terms of image, analogy and metaphor and then from the point of view of developing design strategies which present options or alternatives suitable to various specific programmatic requirements.[10]

The Hotel Berlin is developed in a manner similar to the design of the Enschede project in that it deals with pure geometries. However, it must also be seen as a solution which tries to reintroduce into this area of Berlin the spatial definition it had prior to the destruction of World War II. The Hotel Berlin, together with the proposal for an apartment complex to the northwest of the hotel, would reintroduce to the Lutzowplatz the hardedged definition it once had. The hotel primarily explores building typologies and historical antecedents relating to circular forms which are set within a square. The elements of this project are identified by Ungers as constituting a mini-city, complete with towers, perimeter wall, grand hall, enclosed garden and inner-block court—all examples of typological categories that he uses to illustrate the subjectively identified building types which constitute the formal history of urban architecture in Berlin.[11]

The new state library project for Karlsruhe, the Badische Landesbibliothek, better illustrates the multi-layered nature of Ungers's design process. In Karlsruhe, Ungers's library patently reflects many of the formal and qualitative characteristics which are to be found in the major public structures of the city. In this way it acknowledges the strict heirarchy which one encounters there, for the structure of Karlsruhe owes its form in part to the original plan of 1715 and in part to Friedrich Weinbrenner's additions to the city in the last quarter of the eighteenth century and the beginning of the nineteenth.

3 Museums of Prussian Culture, Berlin-Tiergarten, 1965. O.M. Ungers. Axonometric.
4 Schlossplatz/Museumpark, Braunschweig, 1975. O.M. Ungers. Axonometric.
5 Museuminsel, Berlin. View in 1900.

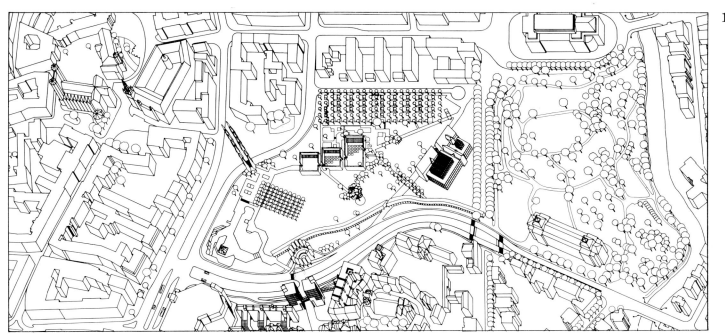

4

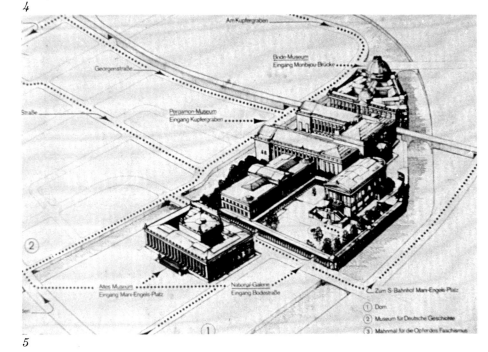

5

6 Baden State Library, Karlsruhe, 1979. O.M. Ungers. Perspective along Erbprinzenstrasse.
7 St Stephan's Church, Karlsruhe, 1803. Friedrich Weinbrenner.

Ungers's library is sited to the south of Weinbrenner's St. Stephan's church (fig. 7), and is not unlike the buildings that Weinbrenner designed to line the Marktplatz. In the case of the library, as in the Marktplatz structures, the uniform definition of the public spaces is given primary importance through the almost equal treatment of the facades in their linear aspect. However, the architecture of Weinbrenner's church is also referred to by raising the library's central volume to match the nave of the church in profile. Ungers further alludes to elements in the church by creating a central domed area that echoes St. Stephan's Pantheon-like interior. This space becomes the library's central reading area, a main space that one may argue is comparable to the reading room of the British Museum, or to the central volume of Gunnar Asplund's Stockholm Public Library. Ungers pays additional homage to Weinbrenner's typology by developing the plan form of the library in such a way as to resemble Weinbrenner's proposal for a public baths building at the Ettlinger Tor (figs. 8, 9) and also by massing the building in a manner similar to that of Weinbrenner's Dance Palace (fig. 11).

This referential use of conceptual characteristics drawn from historical examples is evident in the way in which Ungers finally articulates his proposals: by not making simplistic replications of historical forms, but rather by redefining modern work in terms of specific historical transformations. In this way Ungers also transforms other typical elements to be found in classical Karlsruhe (fig. 15). Aside from Weinbrenner's Marktplatz the internal library facades also recall Weinbrenner's Langestrasse arcade (fig. 10), particularly in the pergola that lines the interior court, and in the arcades of the building facing the palace which become the arcade along the main facade of the building. Finally, a pedimented nave derived from St. Stephen's becomes the entry off of the urban garden into the library itself.

Another recent project—a proposal for the plaza next to Constantine's Basilica (Konstantinplatz) (1981) in Trier—essentially restores to the Basilica part of the original low-rise structure that enclosed its atrium and at the same time gives a clear structure to the procession into the building, one which now serves the function of a Lutheran church. The attention to detail evident in the proposal which can be

7

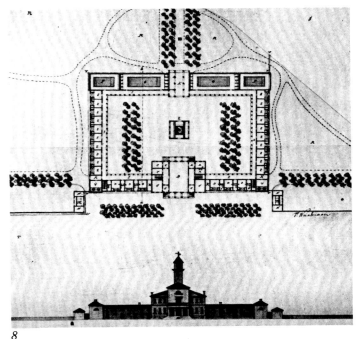

14

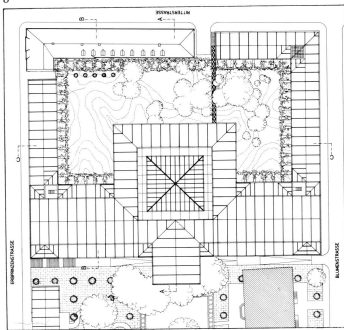

8

9

seen as a re-embodiment of a Roman structure, is consistent with Ungers's concern for that which, finally, results in architecture: the scale, the specific proportions, and the materials used.

The catalogue of forms is endless: until every shape has found its city, new cities will continue to be born. When the forms exhaust their variety and come apart, the end of cities begins. In the last pages of the atlas there is an outpouring of networks without beginning or end, cities in the shape of Los Angeles, in the shape of Kyoto or Osaka—without shape.[12]

The uniqueness of Ungers's design approach derives from his predilection for investigating and exploring the endless possibilities available within what may seem to be a restrictive program. The explorations entered into in his proposals for the parks in Braunschweig, the addition to the Schloss Morsbroich Museum, and his permutational design for a group of houses in Marburg (1976) (figs. 12, 13), as well as the alternatives examined for the Konstantinplatz in Trier, are not idle exercises, but rather experiments that are finally condensed into the summation of a particular solution.

Ungers often explains his ideas by making reference to seemingly unrelated texts, thus further reinforcing the idea of his morphological design process. For example, Ungers may quote, as he has done in his essay "Architecture of the Collective Memory—the Infinite Catalogue of Urban Forms,"[13] from that collection of fantasies which is presented in Italo Calvino's *Invisible Cities*. Ungers uses Calvino's mythical conversations between Marco Polo and Kublai Khan to discuss the idea of the "city of collective memory."

This idea, one that Ungers has been exploring since his projects of the mid-1960's, reflects a continued interest and search for inspiration in a handful of places that are thought to contain the essence of architecture and its evolution, and it is in these places that Ungers finds the concept of transformation. Among these places are the garden of Schloss Glienicke in Berlin (fig. 14), with its structures by Schinkel, Lenne, Persius and others; the garden of Schloss

8 Bad, Ettlinger Tor, Karlsruhe, 1803. Friedrich Weinbrenner. Section and elevation.
9 Baden State Library. Roof plan.
10 Langestrasse arcade (now Kaiserstrasse), Karlsruhe, 1808. Friedrich Weinbrenner. Perspective.
11 Dance Palace, Karlsruhe, 1796. Friedrich Weinbrenner. Section and elevation.

10

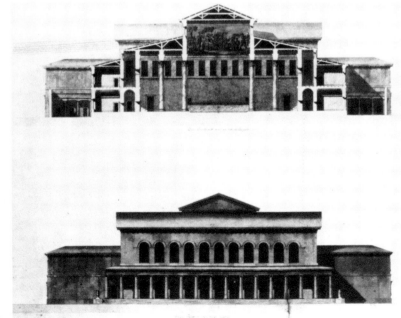

11

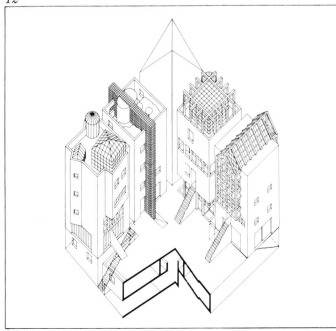

Wörlitz in Weimar; and the cathedral in Trier. These romantic gardens and the cathedral reflect different levels of the same ideal. Glienicke in particular contains elements which were purposefully placed to serve specific functions *and* refer to the evolution and transformation of architectural form. Ungers discusses his ideas of transformation by illustrating how a tree stump at Glienicke changes itself into a column and then into a caryatid; or, from the site, he shows how a ruin is both a hut and a Greek temple, how it is a kind of temple within a temple; or how stones across a brook are transformed into a stone bridge and finally into a pergola as the quintessential form of a bridge across a meadow (fig. 16).[14]

In the cathedral in Trier (fig. 16), on the other hand, an accidental layering of elements is evident, from Constantine's palace which forms the basis of the cathedral's foundations, to the Romanesque, Gothic, and Neoclassical elements, all combined within the cathedral and its cloister. This heterogeneous layering of forms reflects the historical evolution of Germany's oldest city. Ungers seeks to incorporate this idea of transformation into his designs. A typical example of such a transformation is the concept of the "house within a house," found in his project for the German Architecture Museum in Frankfurt (1980), and in the proposed solar houses for Landstuhl (1979), both of which, like traditional Russian dolls, have the quality of being composed of an endless regression of casings. Another strategy is to complement or enforce a dialectical relationship between different parts, as with the "Pyramus and Thisbe" house/office in Berlin-Spandau (1976) (fig. 17).

The Great Khan owns an atlas in which are gathered the maps of all the cities: those whose walls rest on solid foundations, those which fell in ruins and were swallowed by the sand, those that will exist one day and in whose place now only hares' holes gape.[15]

In dealing with an architectural design process that depends on the subjective interpretation of seemingly unrelated sets of concepts and criteria, Ungers is attempting to create an architecture which responds to the collective unconscious;

*12 Ritterstrasse, Marburg, 1976.
O.M. Ungers. Axonometric.
13 Ritterstrasse, Marburg.
Axonometric.
14 Schloss Glienicke, Berlin, 1816,
1826-1827. Karl Friedrich Schinkel.
15 Schlossplatz, Karlsruhe. View of
buildings.*

16 Cathedral, Trier, 13th-18th century (main building period). View of west facade.
17 House and Office, Berlin-Spandau, 1976. O.M. Ungers. Axonometric.

an architecture rich in meaning and references to the history and structure of each particular site.

The city of the "collective unconscious" does exist—it could be any city. The city of the "collective memory," however, has yet to be realized. As of now it only exists in gardens built as cities, in which the recollection of places is meant to be the creative idea: this is the case in the Schlosspark Glienicke...[16]

Notes
1. O.M. Ungers, "Designing with Morphology" (lecture, School of Architecture, University of Oklahoma, Nov. 1977).
2. Reinhard Gieselman; O.M. Ungers, "Towards a New Architecture" in Ulrich Conrads, *Programs and Manifestoes in 20th Century Architecture* (Cambridge: MIT Press, 1970), p.166.
3. Vittorio, Gregotti, "Oswald Mathias Ungers" in *Lotus* 11 (1976), p.12.
4. O.M. Ungers, "Designing and Thinking in Images, Metaphors and Analogies" in *Man-Trans-Forms* (New York: Cooper-Hewitt, 1976), p.104.
5. O.M. Ungers, "Architecture of the Collective Memory—The Infinite Catalogue of Urban Forms" in *Lotus* 24 (1979), p.7.
6. Gerardo Brown-Manrique, "Schloss Morsbroich—Ungers' Museum Project in Leverkusen" in *Architectural Design* vol.50, n.1/2 (Jan./Feb. 1980), pp.8-15.
7. O.M. Ungers, "Urban Intervention: Supreme Court Design for West Berlin, 1979" in *International Architect* vol.1, n.2, (1979), pp.47-60.
8. O.M. Ungers, "Architecture of the Collective Memory" (op.cit.), p.9.
9. Italo Calvino, *Invisible Cities* (New York: Harper & Row, 1972), p.82.
10. O.M. Ungers, "Project for Braunschweig Castle Park" in *Lotus* 14 (1977), pp.100-127.
11. O.M. Ungers, "Concours pour l'Hotel Berlin" in *Architecture d'Aujourd'hui* n.213 (Feb. 1981), pp.52-56.
12. I. Calvino, *Invisible Cities* (op.cit.), p.139.
13. O.M. Ungers, "Architecture of the Collective Memory" (op.cit.), pp.5-11.
14. O.M. Ungers, *Transformations* (Cologne: Studioverlag fur Architecktur L. Ungers, 1981). An excerpt from this book appears in *Architectural Review* vol.169, n.1012 (June 1981), p.363.
15. I. Calvino, *Invisible Cities* (op.cit.), p.137.
16. O.M. Ungers, "Architecture of the Collective Memory" (op.cit.), p.11.

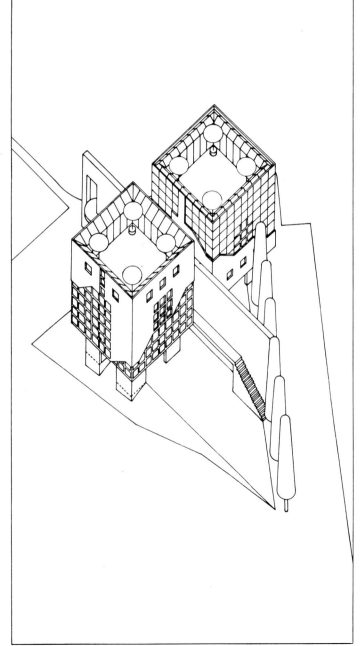

Excerpts from a Dialogue Between Heinrich Klotz and O.M. Ungers

Translated by Jane O. Newman and John H. Smith

Klotz: You were one of the few German architects who participated in the important CIAM *(Congrès Internationaux d'Architecture Moderne)* conventions in Aix-en-Provence from as early as 1954. Since that time you seem to have preserved the international connection that developed there as an act of protest against the doctrines of the Bauhaus and Le Corbusier.

Ungers: It was in Aix-en-Provence that the important and decisive discussions were held that in the end led to the break between the younger and older generations of CIAM. Team X was the result of the break up of the CIAM. The central question debated in Aix-en-Provence was the demand to publicly acknowledge the criteria developed by the older generation under Le Corbusier's direction as universally binding for each and every design. These criteria were work, living, traffic, recreation, and leisure. They created a kind of evaluation matrix against which every design was measured. The result was that all of the designs were for all practical purposes more or less identical, since the same principles were applied in each case. Those designs which did not respect these criteria which for example considered a variety of conditions, could not be judged.

Klotz: And so there was no more "local color;" they had succeeded in eliminating the *genius loci*.

Ungers: Exactly. Instead, an attempt was made to determine a universal law with respect to the necessary criteria. This led to protests by the younger members of the CIAM. They demanded the evaluation of each design according to the individual situation out of which it had been developed. The result was a head-on confrontation and finally a dissolution of the CIAM. And it was this principle, that local conditions and the specific situation had to be respected in design, that became one of the major themes of Team X.

Klotz: And you were involved in this discussion from the very beginning?

Ungers: I participated in the discussions in Aix-en-Provence. Somewhat later in the early sixties, I organized a Team X conference in Berlin, and I have worked closely with the group ever since.

Klotz: Has this phalanx of architectural theorists been able to stay together until the present time?

Ungers: There was in fact something like a second splinter group within the Team X group, or perhaps it would be better to say, another line of discussion that revealed massive intellectual differences. It took place in 1959 in Otterlo, Holland, when Ernesto Rogers displayed his Torre Valasca building in Milan. Rogers not only accommodated local conditions on the social, architectural and traffic levels, but went one step further to absorb the city's historical tradition into his architecture. He sought a direct historical reference point and incorporated historical precedents into the new design. This led to a sharp confrontation between Rogers and Peter Smithson, who, with the support of his colleagues, rejected this kind of historical citation. He understood it incorrectly as far as I am concerned. Smithson, however, accepted the idea later. For example, in his publication on Bath, he considered historical elements together with the architecture and tried to fill them with new content. Thus, my own designs must of course be seen in terms of the background of these debates, first in Aix-en-Provence on considering local conditions and then in Otterlo on the role of historical tradition. It became clear to me that architects must recognize contexts and the historical continuity which determines the identity of any specific site and from which a new architecture necessarily develops. It would be pointless once again to search for some sort of universal style which exists only in the abstract, independent of time and place.

Klotz: You once mentioned that you became aware of [the] principle of strict regularity which allows for rich variation upon observing Karl Friedrich Schinkel's buildings.

Ungers: The fundamental principle of design which distinguishes many of my projects is precisely this notion—that is, I repeat the same element in many interpretations. This principle does indeed originate with Schinkel, whose most striking and successful demonstration of it is the Glienicke Palace in Berlin. The morphological interrelationships are there, but one must really discover them. Of course Schinkel himself never wrote a work concerning them. For example, in the park of the Glienicke Palace one practically stumbles over a golden lion on top of a bridge pile and is at first totally perplexed as to why it is there. Then, a bit further on, one discovers a bridge constructed of unfinished wood which crosses a small stream with overgrown banks. In the end, one finds a whole series of bridges, of interpretations of bridges and their relationships to running water at various points of natural control. There is one bridge constructed in stone which spans a very regulated water artery. Another bridge in cast-iron—cast-iron was, in Schinkel's day, the most technically perfected method of bridge-building—crosses over a canalized river. Suddenly, the interrelationships within this morphological series become apparent; they lead from the primitive earth dam and the simple wooden bridge to the pile bridge on which the gold lion stands. A second example: there are a number of tree trunks spread throughout the park, like so many fragments in the landscape. Further along there are fragments of hewn stone to be discovered on the ground, then an arrangement of fragments of column capitals and bases, next a wall constructed of fragments, and then finally a complex of buildings that seem to be constructed out of a collection of fragments—a Florentine country house and a classical palatial structure. Suddenly one observes an entire spectrum of interpretations of a single theme.

Klotz: They are variations of increasing refinement and articulation of a leitmotif. Multiplicity with a great variety of details is created in this way.

Ungers: Exactly. And this is very important when one is dealing with architectural quantities. Take a path, a wall, or a structure: each of these elements permits a series of interpretations. Not every path is the same. A path can be a playing path, an allée, an arcade, or a gallery. There are any number of possibilities. Numerous interpretations can be found to fulfill one and only one function. It is a procedure by means of which the scope of design can be enriched; a wide scale of possible interpretations made even wider, and employed according to the demands of the specific conditions of the preexisting situation. In the end, it is this vocabulary which is at one's disposal in the production of the design. A writer, for example, does not have merely a single word at his disposal, but can express the same idea in a variety of ways.

Klotz: In all of these ideas you are reaching back to the architectural theory of the Renaissance, the very tradition to which Schinkel often appealed. The principle of diversity was developed and used in a conscious way for the first time by Leon Battista Alberti. So in effect we shouldn't even speak of a principle, but rather of a fundamental doctrine of humanism. It contradicts the law of series in a fundamental way and of course assumes individuality. The doctrine of diversity contradicts standardization, which promises at most a limited multiplication and a simple concept of repetition, and functions as a stumbling-block on the way to a purely functional and materials-oriented architectural technology. Diversity is the objectification of a human psychological need—we experience constraint in uniformity, and the hope of freedom in a confrontation with diversity.... It is [sometimes] said that architecture, like every technological discipline, is a matter of optimalization. We forget, however, that it is an element of the human universe as well and thus has an effect on the psychological sphere.

Ungers: And we also forget that man cannot be optimized. For if it were true that architecture could be optimized, we would have to assume that man could be optimized as well. But human wishes, dreams, and desires are so important and so diverse that we must provide a certain amount of space to accommodate them. When architecture allows itself to be technologized, it goes in a completely false direction. The figure of the construction specialist takes the place of the architect as the formative spirit who allows his ideas and dreams to penetrate the design. This type of person sees himself as an engineer and an organizer. Architects who design prefabricated systems insist over and over again that the various parts of the system can be arranged in a variety of ways. They act as if they were nothing more than organizers or simply spectators. They discover a system that is based on a square or on some other geometrical form and then they are free to do with it whatever they desire. Architecture simply ceases to exist at that point, for it signifies that the architect has given up his individuality and no longer understands himself as the one who locates a form or determines how the space will be formed. He is no more than a technical assistant who participates in the process purely as an onlooker and influences the system only in an anonymous and functional way. He organizes it and utilizes it; he is no more than a manipulator.

Klotz: But couldn't the architect then be tempted to make himself stand out in some other way, by using innovative forms for example? He might be tempted to seek out the opposite extreme and, in the face of an anonymous system of optimalization, attempt to identify himself by means of individualistic virtuoso twists.

Ungers: In my opinion, the architect, on a limited primary level, must make some basic kinds of decisions when it is a matter of urban space, the square and the street, or the structure of the building in a more generalized context. These are commitments to certain principles that must be made at some point. They cannot be deduced from some arbitrary construction system. And yet, these kinds of systematic structures can be seen everywhere. It is simply wrong for architects to content themselves with the conviction that they only need to develop or to settle on a system, and everything else can simply be derived from that system. When an architect does this, he evades his real responsibility. There is a preexisting situation from which and within which he must make certain decisions. It has always been this way in architecture, even in an ancient architecture like that of the Greeks, who worked with simple, established elements. Just consider how decisive the determination of the location of the relationship to the surrounding landscape was for a Greek temple. It is the architect's duty. In this case he must assume total responsibility in my opinion.

Klotz: I have noticed that in all of your designs since about 1955, you have denied the general principle which most architects adopted at that time; that is, dealing with large uniform structures which, according to the theory of Ludwig Mies van der Rohe, for example, were a series of single blocks that simply had to be set in order next to one another. Instead, as early as the German reconstruction, you proceeded to fragment the large forms and thereby create "clusters" of smaller, individuated forms. That was the beginning of what is now a widespread principle of design.

Ungers: A principal grew out of these elements—the stepped and the set-back structures, the loosely flowing architectonic spaces and whatever else belonged to these designs—a principle which was adopted by numerous architects. I myself sought a geometric spatial character in my later designs.

Klotz: I assume that this was already a reaction against the Hans Scharoun school which dominated German architecture, especially in Berlin. It certainly would be incorrect to confuse your designs with the results of so-called "organic buildings."

Ungers: Yes, that would certainly be a mistake, one which even Nikolaus Pevsner made when he compared my building in Cologne to those of German Expressionism.

Klotz: Pevsner wrote that in 1959.

Ungers: At that time I hadn't the slightest idea what architectural Expressionism was all about. Afterwards I grew very interested in the topic and dealt with it extensively.

Klotz: Pevsner was, after all, a declared enemy of Expressionism.

Ungers: Yes, and he considered me one of those who was continuing in the tradition of German Expressionism. But I did not have the slightest historical preference for, or stylistic ambitions concerning Expressionism. My designs have nothing to do with Expressionism; my architectural plans have nothing to do with the metaphysical conceptions which are a part and parcel of Expressionism nor with the spiritual fanfare which accompanies it. Neither my building in Cologne, nor the Oberhausen College, nor the earlier projects is related to Expressionism. Of course, my work thus far does reflect a variety of qualities. On the one hand, there are designs which are severe and rational; on the other hand, the emotional element naturally plays a certain role as well. Some buildings are characterized by loosely integrated, less formally arranged rooms. But the important thing is that both sides should be recognized as parts of a whole, not as isolated features.

Klotz: You have also turned against Scharoun and his school because he robbed architecture of its severity. You offer a new firmness as opposed to his irregular ground plans.

Ungers: When I arrived in Berlin in the sixties to study architecture, Scharoun's influence was virtually tyrannical and unchecked. His formal language was being applied in an epigonic fashion. I rejected the way in which certain of his followers formalistically exploited a principle which had developed earlier, under different conditions and out of a specific philosophical conception. Another objection was more fundamental and was directed against Scharoun himself, who actually always denied the idea of the city. This was most obvious in his design for the capital city, Berlin. There he interpreted the city as a countryside and spoke of the "park-city" and the "countrified area of culture." This was evident as well in the Philharmonic Hall, where he referred to "vineyards" instead of rooms. I, on the other hand, was much more interested in creating clearly defined urban spaces and propagating an urban architecture, and this led me to oppose the Scharoun school. These positions occasionally become polemical. Naturally, I established a position which was contrary to Scharoun's and sought a rational approach to architecture. I opposed the dissolution of the city into a countryside with my formulation of strictly delineated urban spaces and the definition of clearly determined forms.

Klotz: What distinguished Scharoun from his followers?

Ungers: I believe that Scharoun developed his ideas from the tradition of German Expressionism. In the twenties, there was a lively discussion concerning shapes and forms which were based on anthroposophism. However Scharoun's followers simply dropped this philosophical framework and adopted the forms without reflection. This style of building and planning was then draped with the cloak of "humaneness:" and was dubbed "democratic architecture" because of its uncontrolled formal language. Then any architecture which employed right angles and rationally determined forms was attacked for being "inhumane." That was a polemic which I could not accept.

Klotz: In the meantime, you attained international recognition for your direction in architecture. Yet today your position has once again created enemies who condemn it graphically with the term "Brutalism" (*Brutalismus).*

Ungers: In the Anglo-American world, "New Brutalism" has a different meaning than *Brutalismus* does in Germany.

Klotz: We understand *Brutalismus* to mean the harsh brutality of concrete (Beton-Brutalismus).

Ungers: That is definitely a misinterpretation of the term. Of course, there is also a certain irony at work here. "Brutalism" *(Brutalismus)* was originally a provocative term and implied something like "brutal honesty," which had something to do with an ethical standpoint. It was more of a moral question than a stylistic one, then it turned quickly into a stylistic interpretation. Finally, in Germany at least, the term came to be used only in formalistic contexts. Our demands—and that once again goes back to the CIAM discussion—were to idealize nothing and to attempt only that which is possible within the parameters of the given situation. In other words, to not beautify, nor mask, nor strive for dishonest civility; to not cover anything up, but to make a statement as directly as possible. At the superficial level, this principle led me to the point that I photographed my buildings only in the rain so as not to falsely emphasize their beauty in publications. I thought that the buildings should be able to stand up to dripping water and a gray background. If the idea of Brutalism is really pursued logically, it is obvious that the questions of urban architecture, of dealing with preexisting elements, and of interpreting certain situations—that is, the question of "knitting and fitting" to quote Peter Smithson, or what I called an "architecture as if discovered"—actually have their origins in the early phase of Brutalism. There are, of course, many architects in Germany who simply exploit the results of these efforts for an aesthetic effect, without understanding the actual philosophical background of the movement. Therefore, it is indeed important to correct the usage of the term Brutalism, since most critics apply it as a deprecatory concept. In my development and that of most of my friends, Brutalism marked a decisive intellectual stance, for it provided an escape from the International Style of the twenties.

This text was first published in *Architektur in der Bundes republik* (1977).

Hotel Berlin

Berlin 1976

Located on a main axis from the Tiergarten and connecting with the Klingelhoferstrasse, the Hotel Berlin project is highly responsive to the existing city fabric, including the famous Lützowplatz, which it would effectively help to restore by defining one of its sides. In fact, a landscaped restoration of the historic space of the square is one of the corollaries of the project itself, including the low-level definition of the square by an arcade and the replacement of the historic rondel, complete with a fountain, on the axis of the Tiergarten's Grosser Stern. This diagonal axis will be emphasized by the completion of an avenue which is already partially built.

The formal motif of the restored Lützowplatz—a circle within a rectangle—will also be repeated in the *parti* of the hotel, thereby symbolically reinforcing a reading of the hotel as a metaphor for the city—*Das Haus als Stadt-Die Stadt als Haus*. A leftover triangular section of the site, bounded by the Kunfurstenstrasse and the Kingelhoferstrasse will be treated as a heavily-planted parterre or grove and used incidentally for parking for 100 cars. This reserved plot could in the future be used as a site for an apartment block.

The height of the hotel has been limited to nine stories in order to not overwhelm other structures in the vicinity, and a clear and tranquil geometric form has been adopted in order to offset the urban chaos of the surrounding area.

The projected development has been conceived of as an urban hotel with an arcaded perimeter. In addition to this, a full height, top-lit rectangular reception hall opens off the Kunfurstenstrasse frontage and thus presents itself as a year-round town square or forum in what is otherwise a relatively unattractive urban environment. While the traditional typological and representative values of the Grand Hotel are alluded to in the arcades and the larger interior public volumes, the exterior is rendered as an urban block rather than a freestanding hotel.

The reception hall at one end of the complex is the focal point of the hotel and all the public circulation of the lower floor refers back to this rectangular volume. While it is possible to enter directly into the reception hall from three sides, the fourth leads to the cocktail bar and to a whole sequence of ground floor restaurants which are arranged around the circular kitchen in the very center of the complex. The kitchen is served from a sub-basement while its roof doubles as the platform for the central garden court. At the same time, on the first floor administration level the reception hall, animated by escalators, connects into an orthogonal grid of interior "streets." These streets lead to elevator/stair lobbies and to various bars and conference rooms placed on the mezzanine at the mid-point of the two-story restaurant volumes. Finally the perimeter arcade helps to link the space of the reception hall to the rest of the composition. The reception hall has shops arranged around its entire perimeter and many of these are accessible from the street as well as from the interior.

The perimeter restaurants are placed so that in fine weather they can easily expand along two sides onto a temporary "cafe-terrace" organized on yet another ring outside the public arcade, complete with awnings and seating alcoves formed by hedges. These rustic dining places face out over flanking lawns; in one instance (the self-service restaurant and the grill room) onto the Lützowplatz and in another (the city restaurant) onto the Shillstrasse.

On the seventh floor of the hotel there is a small health club adjoining the hotel roof garden. This club is equipped with a small swimming pool and a series of exercise rooms.

The hotel's residential accommodations are basically divided into three different types according to their location in the complex: studio rooms on the outer perimeter facing all four points of the compass, studio rooms on the inner circumference of the cylinder facing down into the central garden court, and studio rooms which are stacked on the upper three floors of the reception hall and which receive light from the vitreous roof above.

If and when the hotel is fully developed it will provide a total of about 1200 rooms, although well over half of these could be shut off in blocks as part of a seasonal closing program. The general positioning of stairways and elevators on the

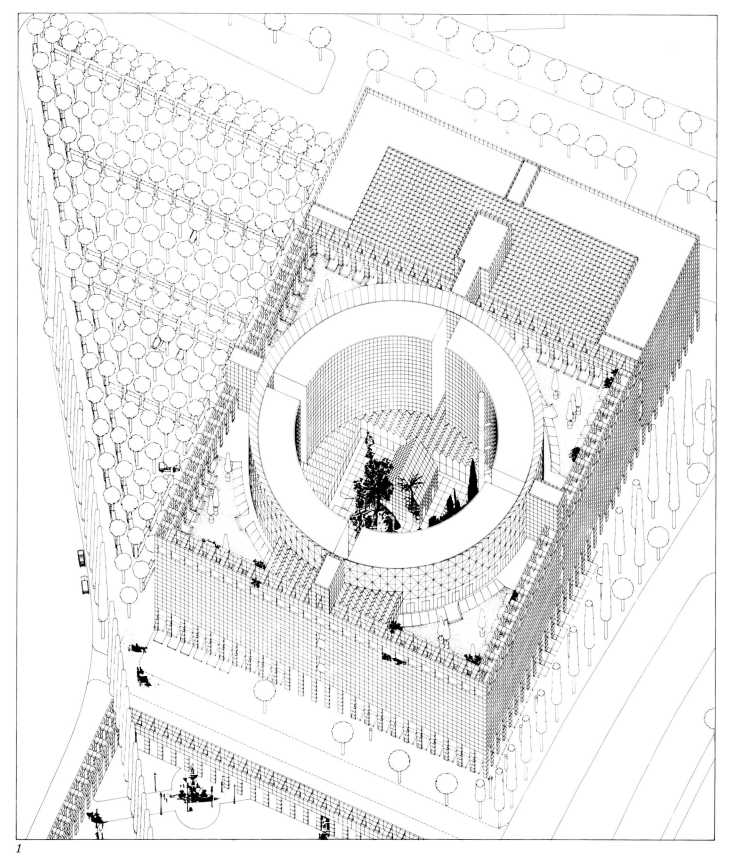

Hotel Berlin

*1 Hotel Berlin, Berlin, 1976.
Axonometric.
2 Block plan.
3 Site plan.
4 Ground floor plan.
5 Second, third and fourth floor plan.*

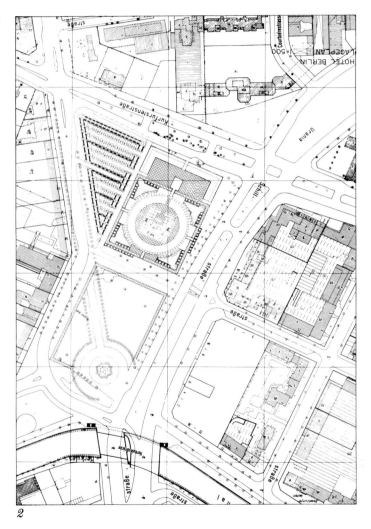

2

primary axes of the cylinder and at the four corners of the enclosing rectangle permits ready access to any of the room blocks.

The general intent is to face the building with a judicious mixture of brick, cinder block, stone panelling and tinted glass, keeping the hues as restrained as possible. The window openings have been optimally placed to satisfy both lighting requirements and the present standards of energy conservation.

The hotel can be conceptually analyzed as a combination of a perimeter wall *(Die Wand)*, a glass-house/reception hall *(Das Glashaus)*, a series of four access towers *(Die Türme)* and finally the inner cylinder or rotunda *(Die Rotunde)*. Aside from this metaphorical analysis, the hotel has also been designed so that it can be both built and operated in sections.

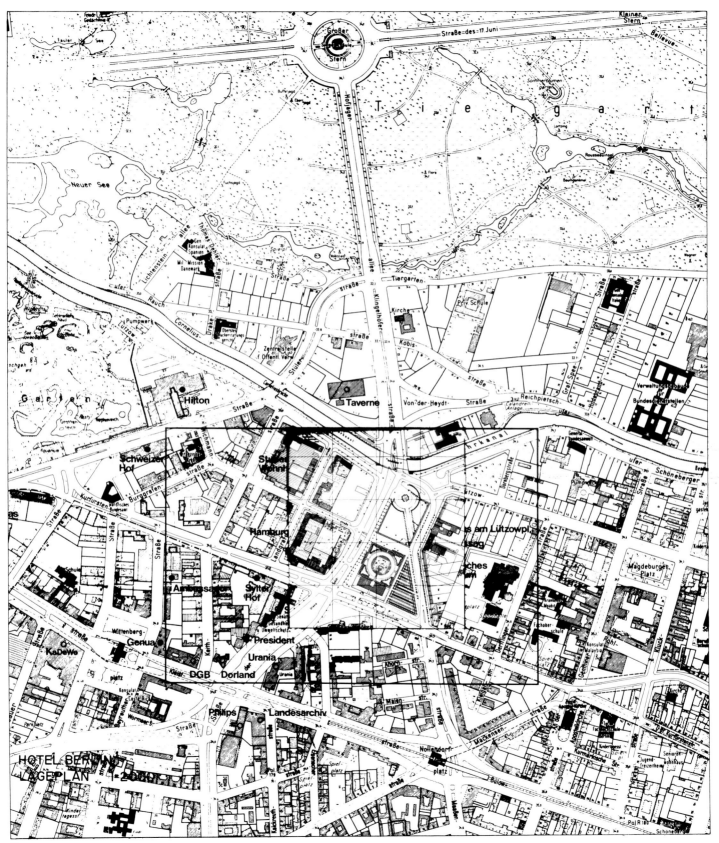

28

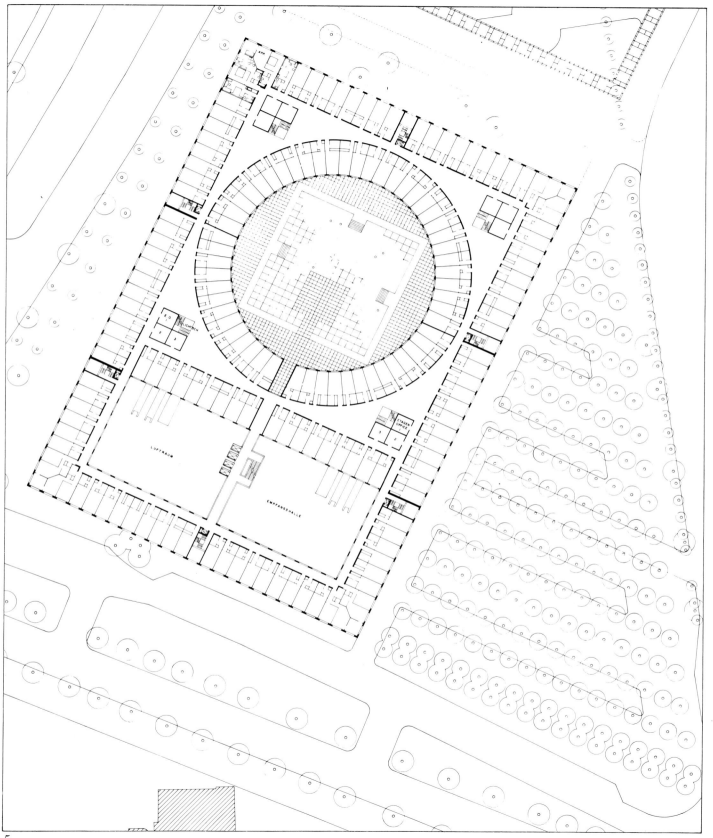

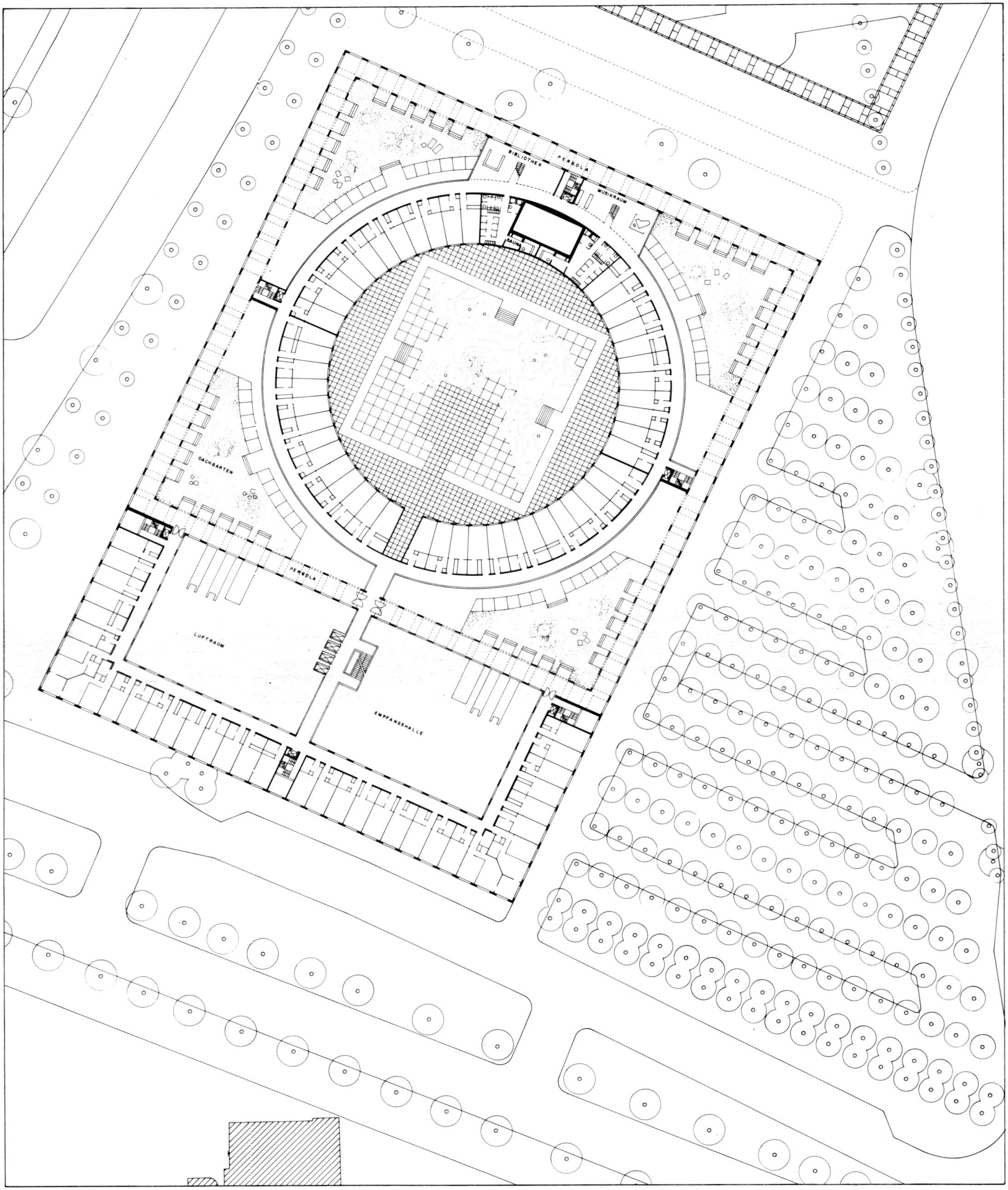
BIBLIOTHEK
PERGOLA
MUSIKRAUM
SAUNA
DACHGARTEN
PERGOLA
LUFTRAUM
EMPFANGSHALLE

6

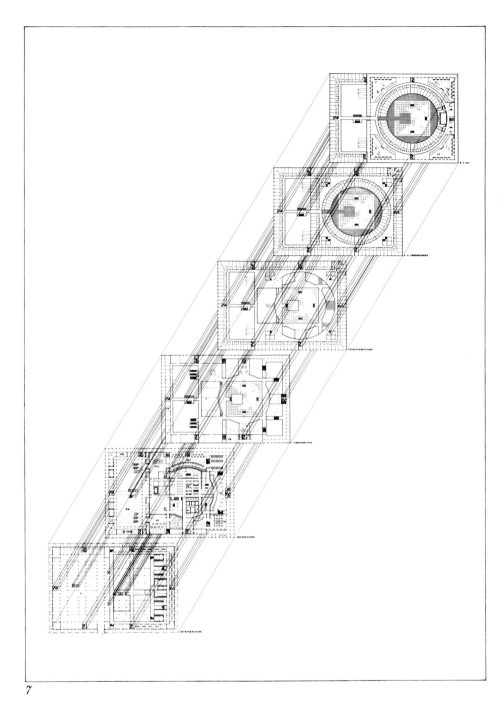

Hotel Berlin

6 Fifth floor plan.
7 Utilization plan.

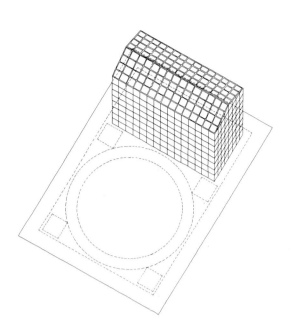

8

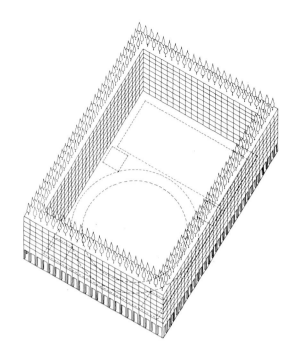

10

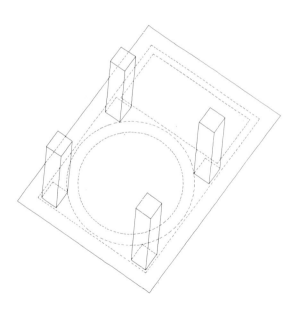

9

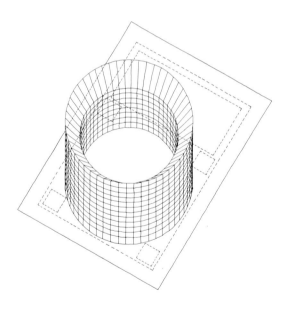

11

Hotel Berlin

8 The Hotel Berlin broken down into generic elements. Glass house.
9 Towers.
10 Wall.
11 Rotunda.
12 "The House in the City— The City in the House."

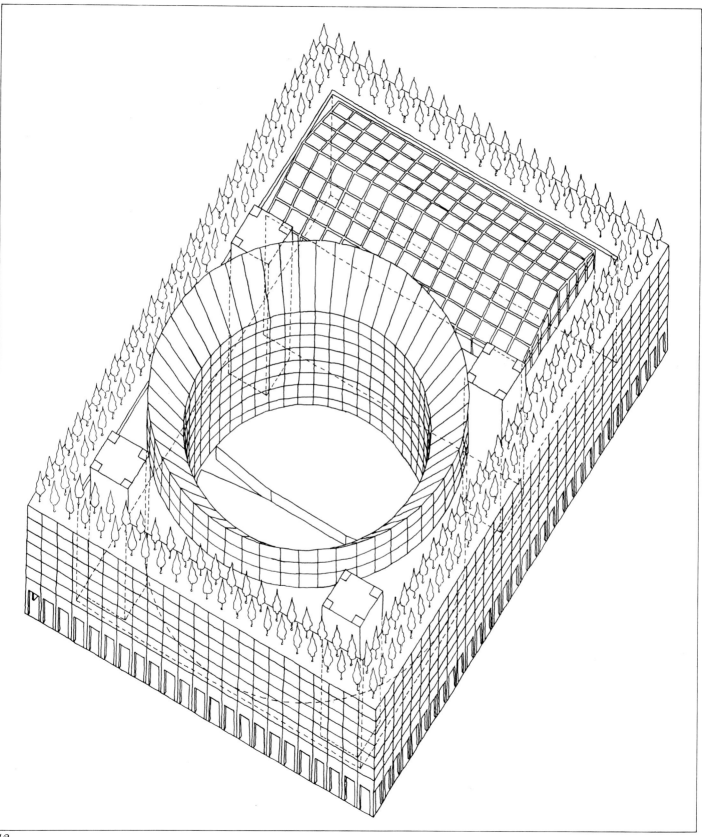

Architecture Museum

Frankfurt on the Main 1978

The site for the Architecture Museum is located on the Schaumainkai in Frankfurt. The museum is part of a larger strategy for urban development known in Frankfurt as the "Museumsufer." The basic idea is to establish a row of museums along the Schaumainkai; a series of institutions which will be created, in part, from existing buildings. The primary concept of the Museumsufer is to provide a new cultural center for the city in the tradition of the old humanistic cultural forum, such as the Museumsinsel built in Berlin during the nineteenth century. We might say that the Museumsufer in Frankfurt will form a kind of museum riverbank. At the same time the existing buildings along the Main will be given a new and more appropriate significance, thereby reinforcing the notion that buildings are historically determined by their location. This general strategy of decentralization seeks to integrate culture, service, business, and residential living.

A *doppelvilla* on a relatively small lot at the corner of the Schaumainkai and the Schweizerstrasse was made available for the Architecture Museum. The villa itself is hardly of great historical or architectural value, for all that it is reputedly based on the architectural form of the Biblioteca Laurenziana. The true value of the villa resides in the contribution it makes to the sense of collective memory which is embodied in the historical fabric of the area. Despite the fact that it would be simpler and less expensive to build a new museum, the commemorative value of the villa justifies its preservation. In general, two basic strategies may be adopted towards the preservation and reuse of existing structures—in the first, the existing spatial subdivision of the building is simply adapted to new uses; in the second, the building is reduced to an exterior shell and a new spatial organization is constructed within.

The first move that was made in the case of the *doppelvilla* was to transform its basic context by surrounding the structure with a wall. With this gesture the house itself became an object on exhibition and thus simultaneously became both an exhibit and an exhibition hall. While its new status as an object represents an alienation, it also imparts a significance to the work which transcends its original purpose.

The existing inner framework of the villa was incompatible with the programmatic requirements of the museum. Thus, the house was gutted, and only its exterior shell was preserved. A new construction was then inserted into the void in order to provide for the necessary exhibition space. The main source of illumination for this space was a light shaft incorporated into the center of the house.

From this basic approach came the architectural theme of a "house within a house," and thus the outer shell, composed of a thick wall of niches, bays and cavities, became comparable to a city wall. The next shell was the house itself, its walls profiled by windows, columns, pilasters and other protrusions. Within this second shell was erected a concrete scaffold and yet another space–form delineated by a filigreed structure filled with glass.

The museum in fact comprises a series of alternating "rooms within rooms," passing from the bounding wall, to the profiled wall, to the inner scaffold, and ultimately to the delicate filigree. This morphological progression of a series of rooms from exterior to interior becomes both the spatial concept and the architectonic theme of the entire museum. The outer shell consists of heavy stone, the profiled wall is made of plaster and stone, the scaffold is cast from poured concrete and the filigree is constructed of steel and glass. The only new elements that are visible from the exterior are the outer wall and the interior filigreed structure which protrudes above the original roof of the villa.

The metamorphosis of the space as an unending movement from exterior to interior allows the visitor to go from an outer to an inner room, which is in turn the outer room relative to the next room, and so on. It is a sequence which cannot be brought to an end and therefore expresses a real and an abstract continuity. The continuity of space itself is the principle informing the concept.

The function of the space and the existing local conditions correspond to this principle, which depends upon the integration, rather than the separation, of contrasts. This idea derives from the *Coincidentia Oppositorum* advanced by the philosopher, Nikolaus von Kues (1401-1464). That is to

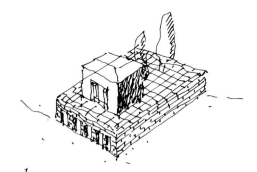

1 Architecture Museum, Frankfurt, 1978. Conceptual sketch.
2 Axonometric.

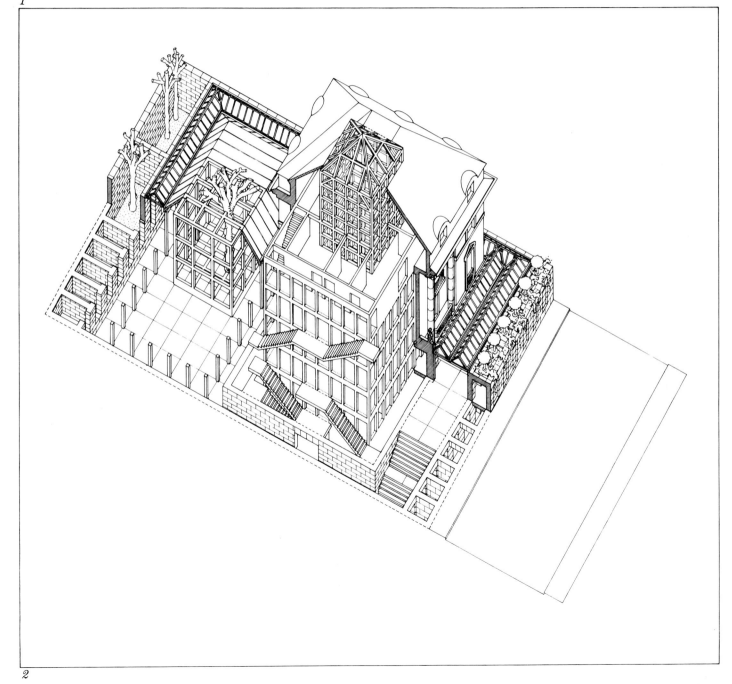

say, the principle of the integration of opposites which are interdependent, rather than their mutual exclusion. The interior court is meant to be understood in this way; as the perfect spatial lattice from which the chestnut tree will spring. This in itself is a commentary on the principle of design, to the extent that the abstract cage contrasts with the natural form of the tree and thereby symbolizes the cerebral in contrast to the natural space. At the same time, it represents the limitation and the unity of these opposites in their morphological interdependence. The overall architectonic concept is also a paradigm for the city. Thus, it should be understood as a spatial microcosm within the macrocosmic urban structure.

Architecture Museum

3 Site plan.
4 Original doppelvilla.
5 Lower ground floor plan.
6 Ground floor plan. Galleries.

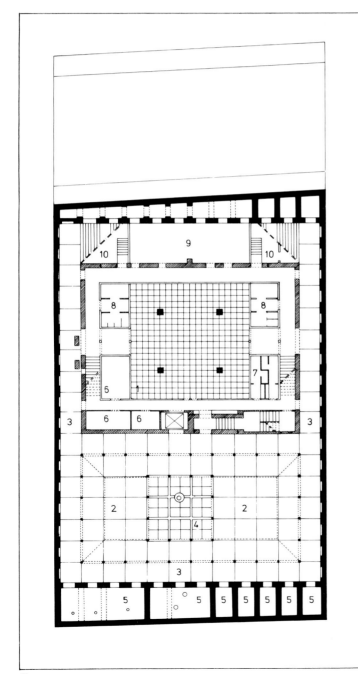
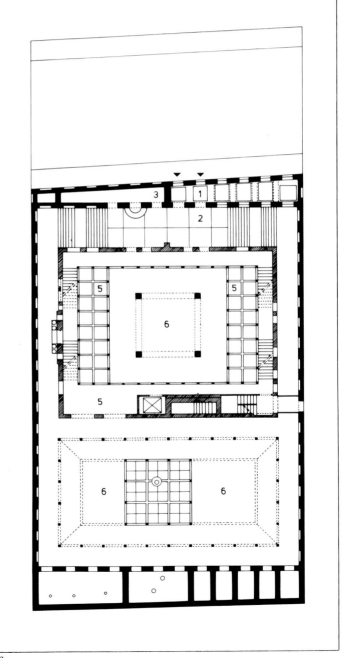

Architecture Museum

7 *First floor plan. Exhibition areas.*
8 *Second floor plan. Cabinets.*
9 *Section.*
10 *Third floor plan. Collections.*
11 *Elevation.*
12 *Fourth floor.*

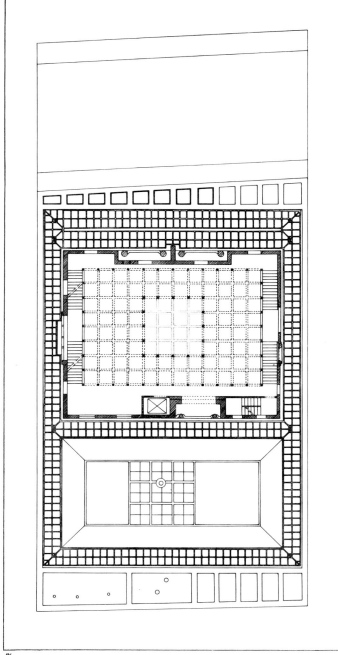

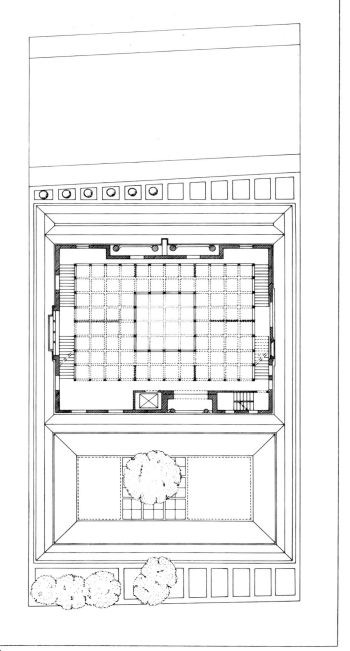

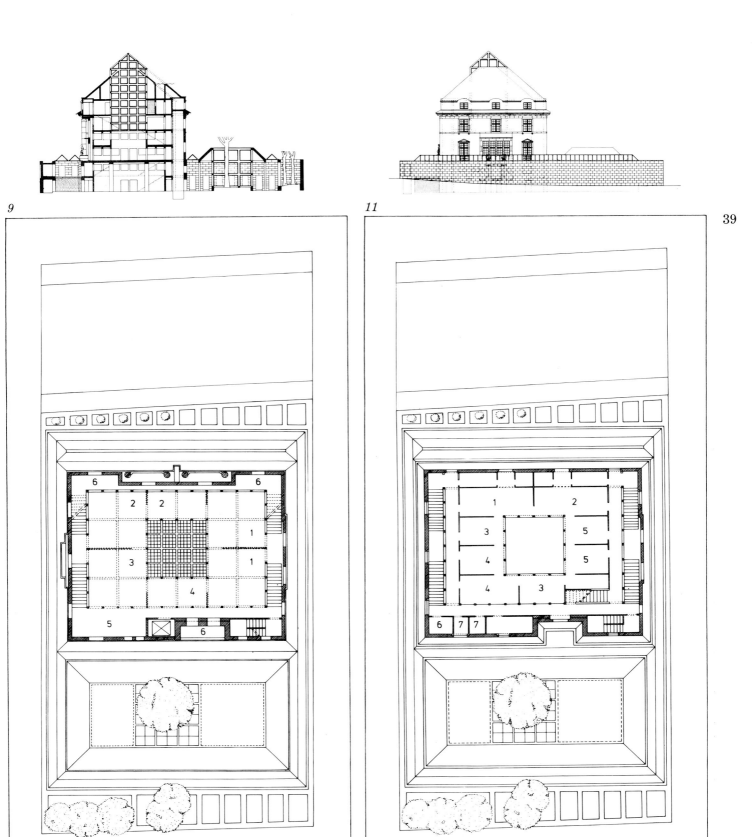

13

15

40

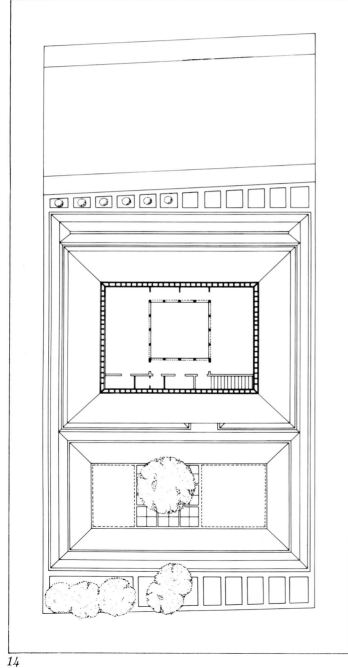

14

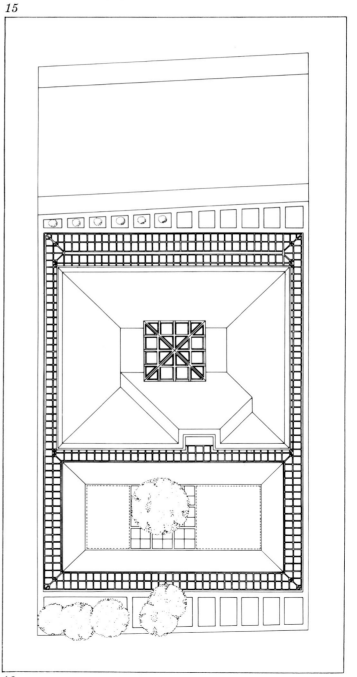

16

Architecture Museum

13 Entrance elevation.
14 Storage rooms.
15 Rear elevation.
16 Roof plan.
17 Interior perspective. Light court, first floor.
18 Interior perspective. Central hall.
19 Interior perspective. Entry hall.

17

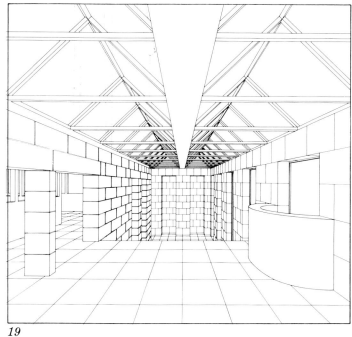

19

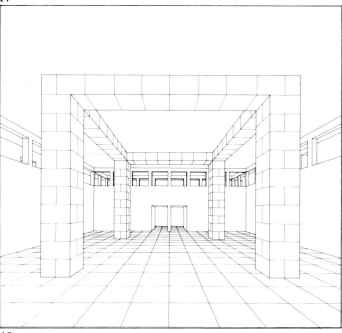

18

Perimeter Block, Schillerstrasse/ Kaiser-Friedrichstrasse

Charlottenberg, Berlin

In this project for the Schillerstrasse and the Kaiser-Friedrichstrasse, an attempt is made to complete the historical urban fabric by relating the new work to the elevations of the adjacent structures and thereby create a unified block. Above all, the existing building on the Kaiser/Friedrichstrasse is incorporated into the new design, in an attempt to preserve an intimate scale, despite an unfavorable orientation and a noisy location.

The vacant space on the lot will be occupied by a structure whose general order derives from the existing building. The organizational scheme of the ground plan duplicates the layout of the existing structure and thus produces an interior court served by four points of the vertical access. The new structure is designed so that all the apartments face onto the quiet courtyard and away from the noise of the Kaiser-Friedrichstrasse and the northerly orientation of the Schillerstrasse. The ground floor is occupied by *maisonettes* with individual entrances, accessible either from the street or from the common courtyard. The older building will be altered to provide apartments similar in quality to those in the new building. The ground floor apartments in the older building are equipped with small front yards which face the inner court. The fourth and fifth floors of the existing block will be converted into *maisonettes* with upper garden courts open to the sky. As with the ground floor apartments, they will be treated like small private houses.

One might call this type of apartment house a city palace (Stadtpalais) in which different types of residential/professional units are integrated into one form, starting with studios for students or elderly people, and ending with large, multi-roomed apartments with separate entrances and gardens for families. These units have also been designed to accomodate office space, including consulting rooms. In this way the mixture of apartments attempts to reflect the complete social spectrum. The interior court not only provides a means of access, but also provides a garden space for the entire house.

The new building will be rendered in plaster following the traditional plaster-faced masonry used in the existing fabric. The roof of the block will be finished in tile and the entire house will stand on a protective two-meter base fabricated of red clinkers.

This combination of fusion and differentiation of old and new structures will be enhanced over time by maintenance and by being painted as a single block.

*1 Perimeter Block, Schillerstrasse
Kaiser-Friedrichstrasse, Berlin,
1978. Axonometric.*

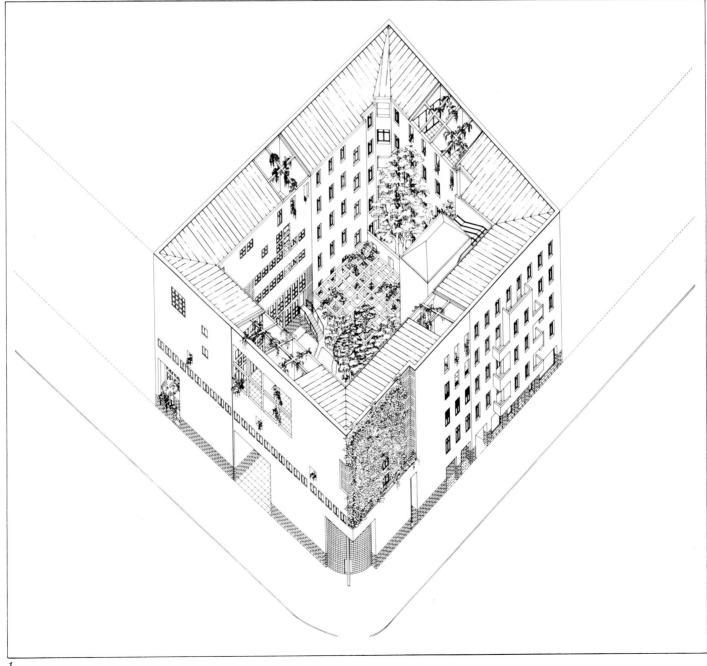

44

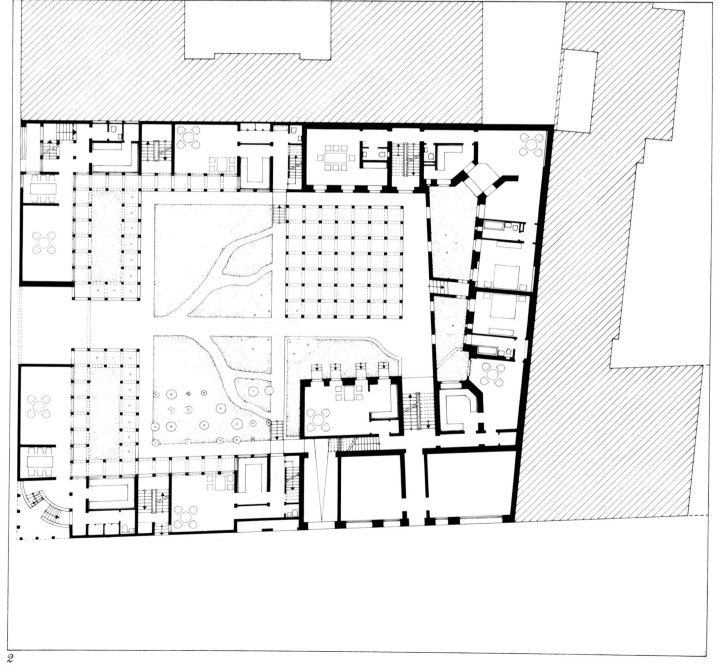

2

Perimeter Block

2 Ground floor.
3 First floor.

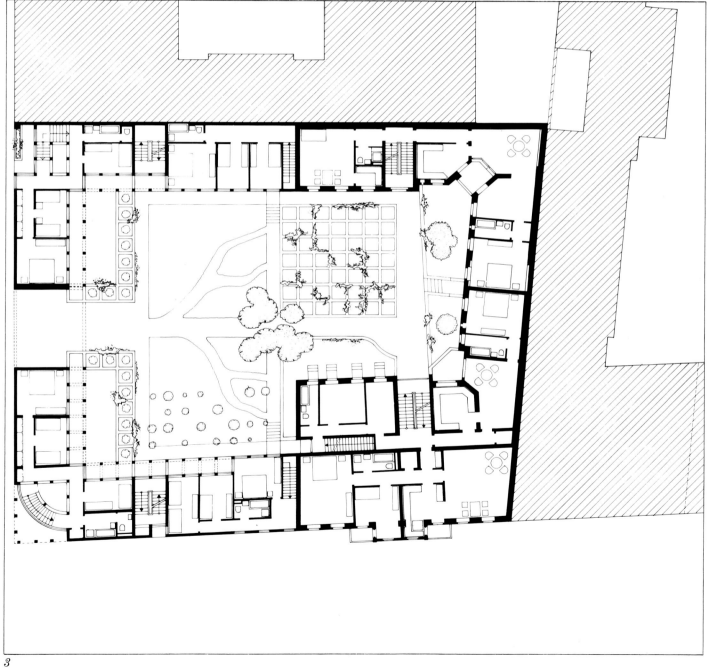

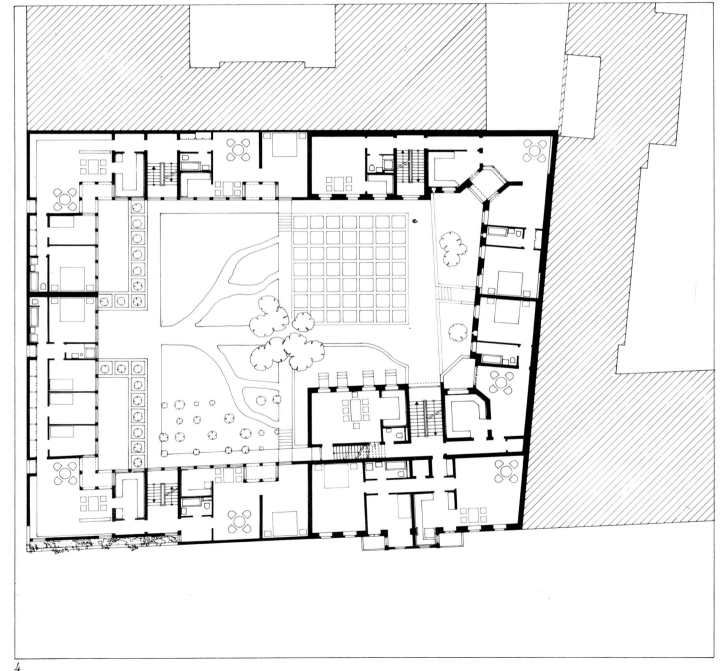

Perimeter Block

4 Second and third floor.
5 Fourth floor.

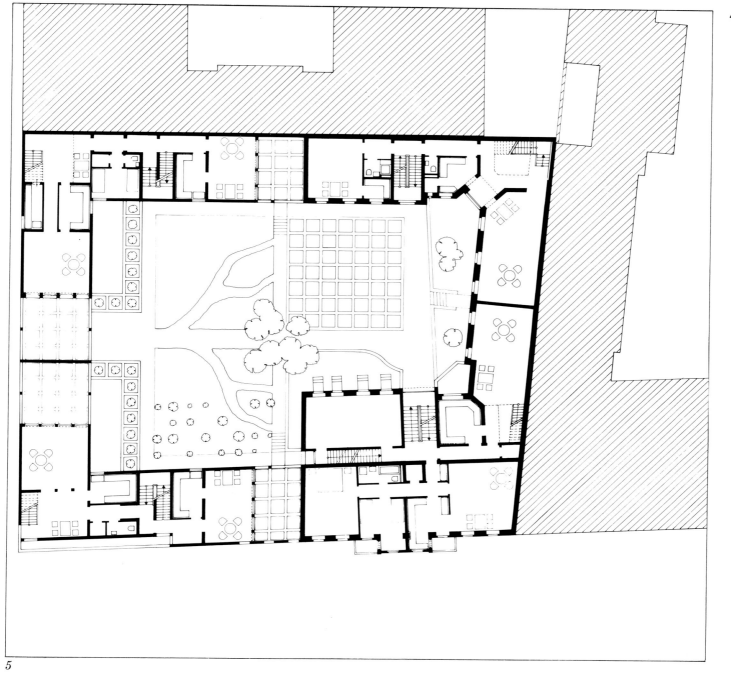

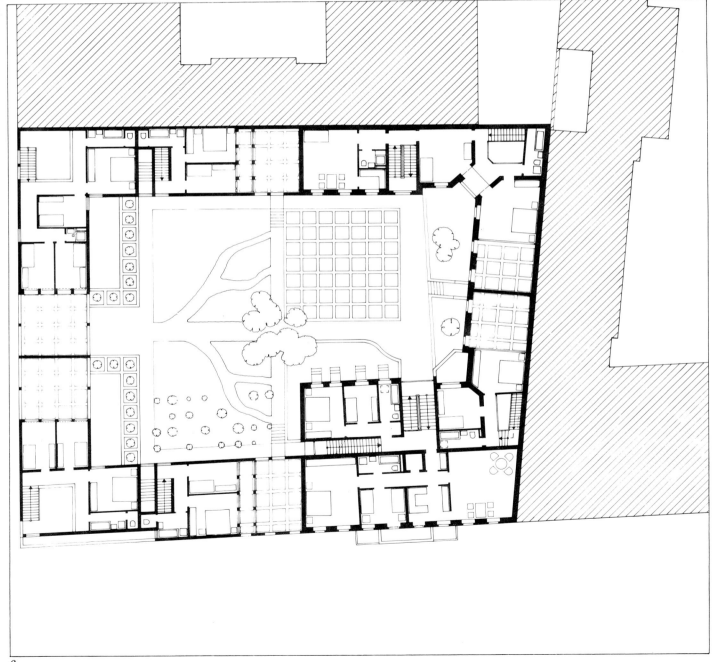

Perimeter Block

6 Fifth floor.
7 North elevation.
8 Section. Inner courtyard, South.

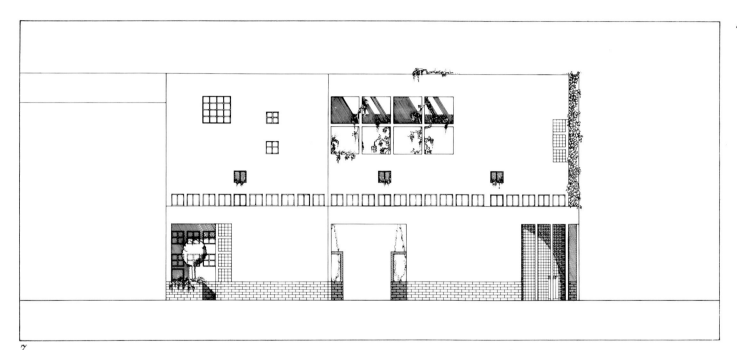

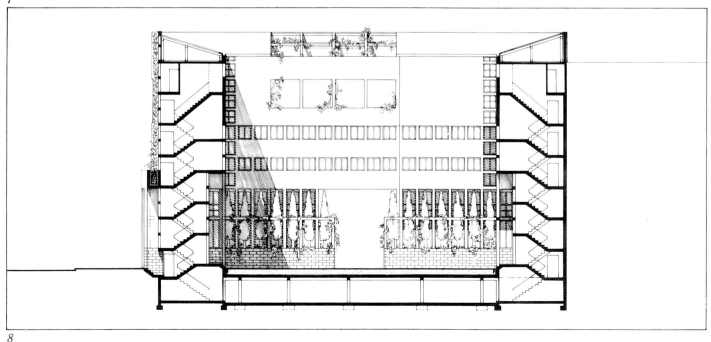

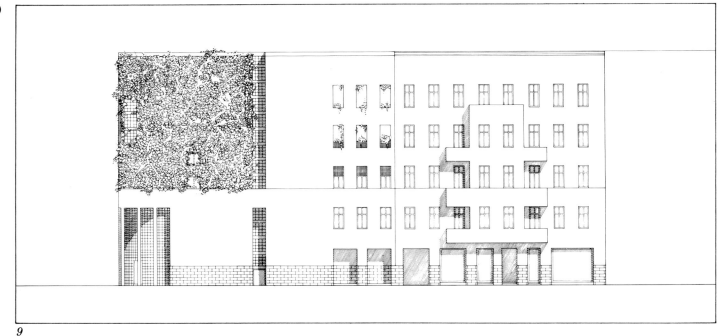

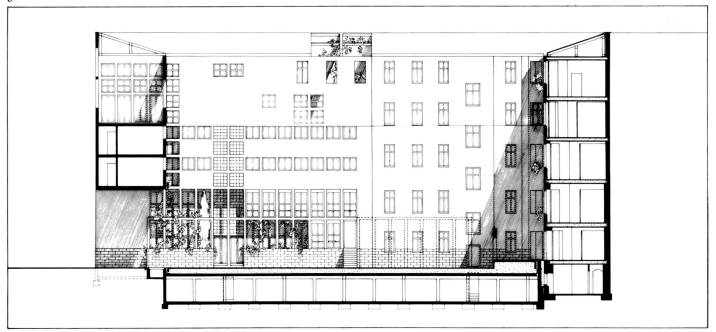

Perimeter Block

9 West elevation.
10 Section. Inner courtyard, West.
11 Section. Inner courtyard, North.

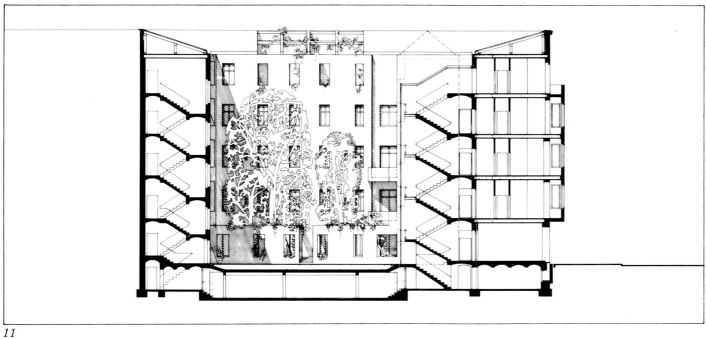

11

Carlsburg Hochschule

Bremerhaven 1979

In accordance with the competition brief, this university extension project in the form of an elongated horseshoe was designed with particular regard for the existing context. The main structure flanks the Karlsburg and is designed to enclose an inner triangular square known as the Karlsplatz. The other sides of this triangular space are to be formed by the Deichstrasse perimeter block along the southeastern edge, and by a cranked block along the northeastern edge, in part paralleling the Fahrstrasse and in part facing out over the Theodor Heussplatz.

The triangular space fulfills the requirement of integrating the university with the pedestrian zone which starts at this point, while the formal intent of the Deichstrasse complex is to simulate the preexisting scale and profile of the old waterfront buildings which once stood on this site. Thus the overall proposal comprises a diverse set of architectural forms which can be justified on many different levels (i.e. educationally, industrially, and residentially).

The new proposal occupies a site bounded by the Karlsburg and extends up to the Deichstrasse where the head of the horseshoe-shaped complex is terminated by the services building, like the bow of a ship pushing towards the shoreline. In this way the project helps to bind the core of the city together with the city theater and the indoor swimming pool.

A rectangular art museum closes the opposite northwestern end of the complex. Within the overall mass, the school itself and the art museum are connected by a sculpture garden immediately above the ground level, which is devoted to the main entrance and parking for 114 cars. This garden, in which marine objects may also be exhibited, overlooks the Karlsplatz as a kind of public balcony and is physically linked to the latter by a stairway.

The principal teaching units are organized around a central longitudinal light court with the larger laboratories being accommodated along the central spine of the raised ground floor. These labs are of varied height and are lit from above.

At grade, the main sidewalk and drive-through passage lead to the main entry, the principal stair hall and the semicircular *mensa*. This inner laboratory "core," covered with a space frame, is organized on a strict modular grid and may be flexibly subdivided. The smaller laboratories and research offices are arranged around the outer perimeter of the horseshoe. The administration offices are located on the top floor, which has a lower ceiling height than the other floors. The first floor above ground level provides for two projecting lecture halls which cantilever out over the *mensa*.

Thus, at the horseshoe end of the building the main services are housed on top of one another as follows: central cafeteria area *mensa*, lecture halls, seminar rooms, and a library. The entrance hall and main stairwell constitute a forum-like space that extends over several floors. This central volume can be used in conjunction with larger events, such as student forums, rallies, theater performances and parties.

The proposed exterior facing is the same type of brickwork as the surrounding buildings on the Theodor Heussplatz and the Fahrstrasse. While making certain subtle nautical references, the building is also intended to function as a type of entrance gate to the Karlsburg which is the main street of Bremerhaven.

In order to provide for certain energy-saving requirements requested in the program, a thirty-square-meter surface suitable for solar energy collection has been incorporated in the roof. Aside from this, the building has been given as compact a form as possible, with the least amount of exterior surface. The energy proposal for the roof over the court is based on the following considerations:
1. Given the optimal use of closed geometry, which facilitates a considerable reduction in the exterior surface of the building, heat loss through transmission will be similarly reduced;
2. the roof over the courtyard can be treated as a heat absorber for solar energy and can thereby help extensively in saving basic energy. By applying passive solar principles (the greenhouse effect) in conjunction with active systems (heat recovery, the application of the principles of the heat pump, etc.) a hybrid system is produced that can, for the most part, cover annual heating and hot water demands;

*1 Carlsburg Hochschule,
Bremerhaven, 1979. Axonometric.*

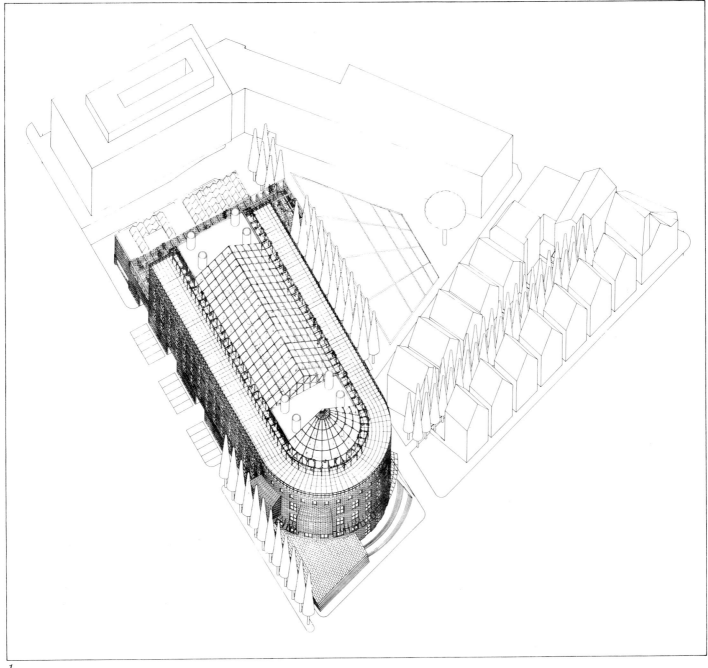

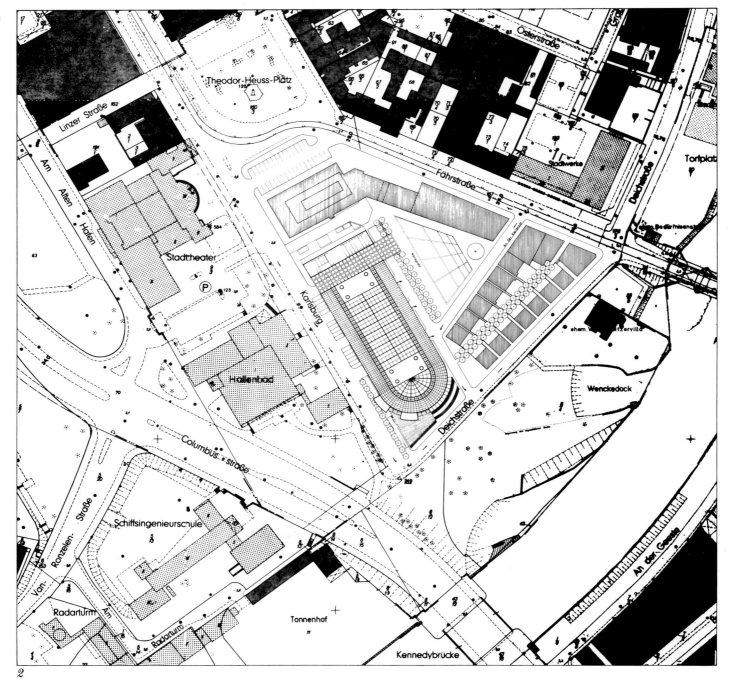

Carlsburg Hochschule

2 Site plan.
3 Basement plan.

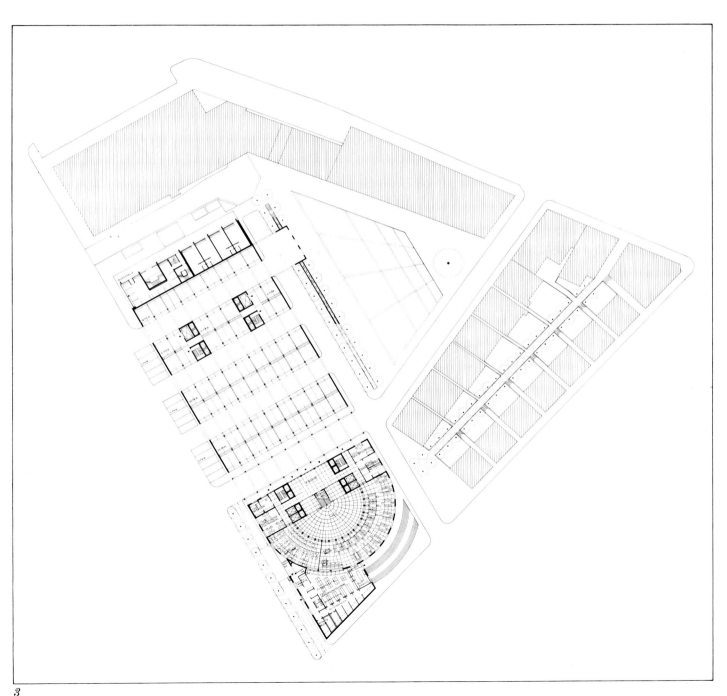

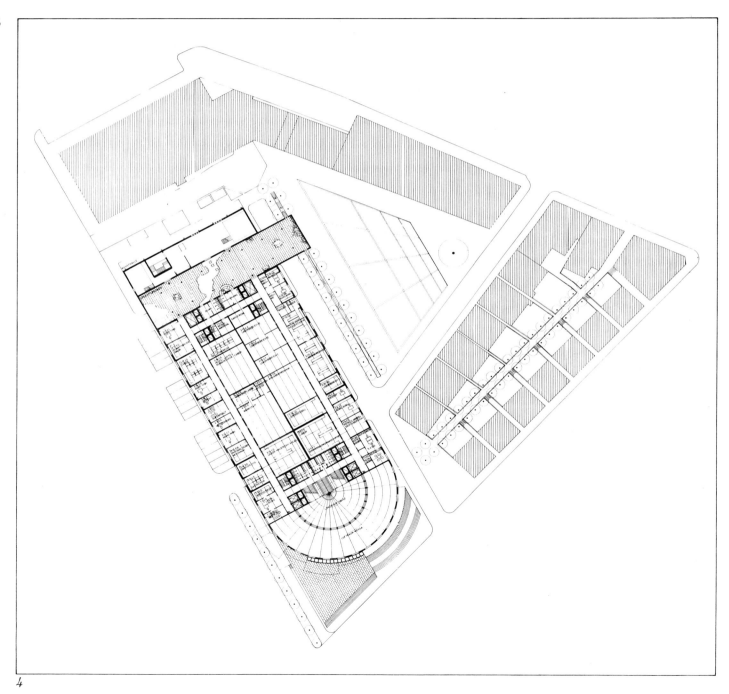

Carlsburg Hochschule

4 Ground floor plan.
5 First floor plan.
6 Second floor plan.
7 Third floor plan.
8 Roof plan.

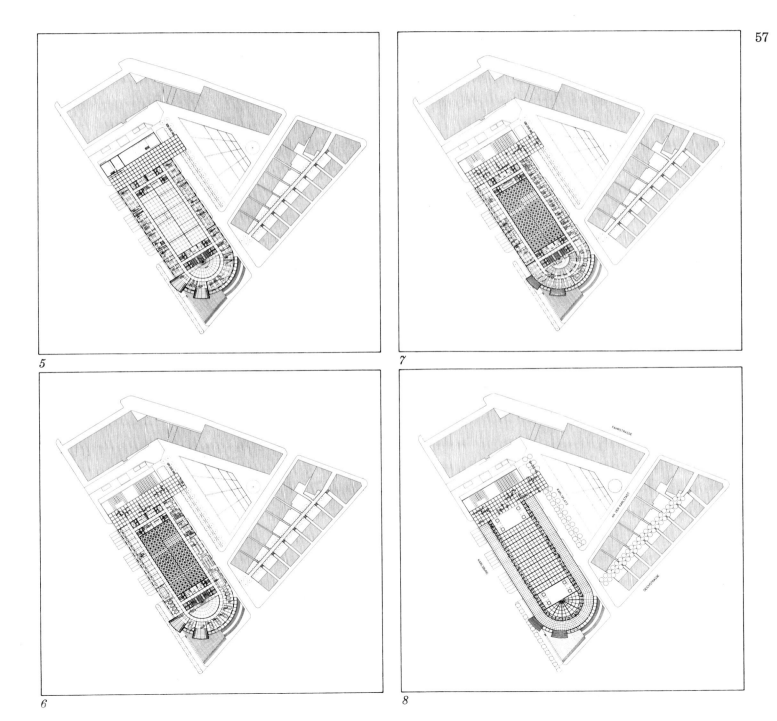

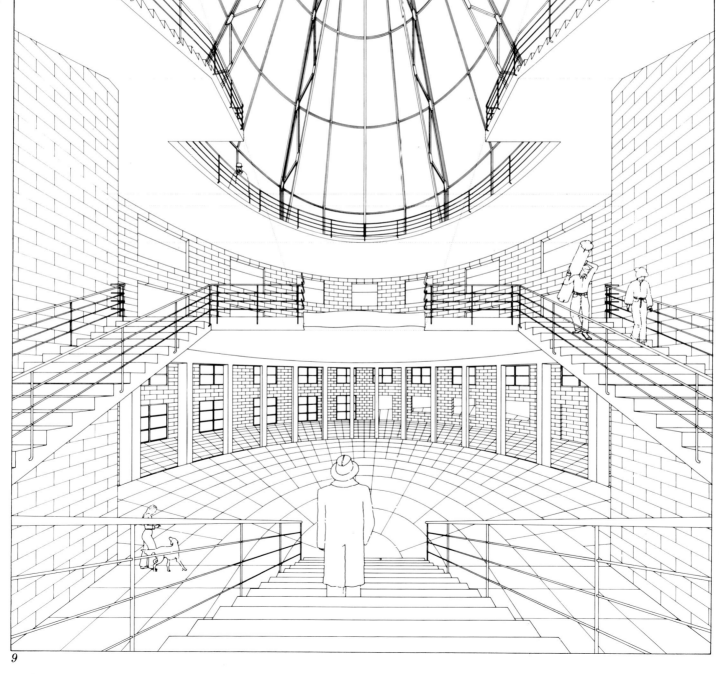

Carlsburg Hochschule

9 Perspective.
10 Section.
11 Left: energy concept diagram;
center: south/east elevation; right:
north/west elevation.

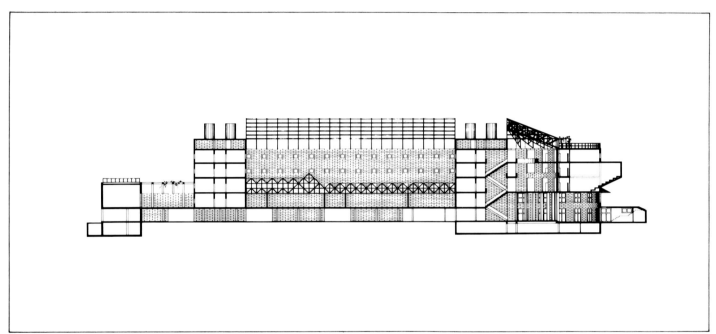
10

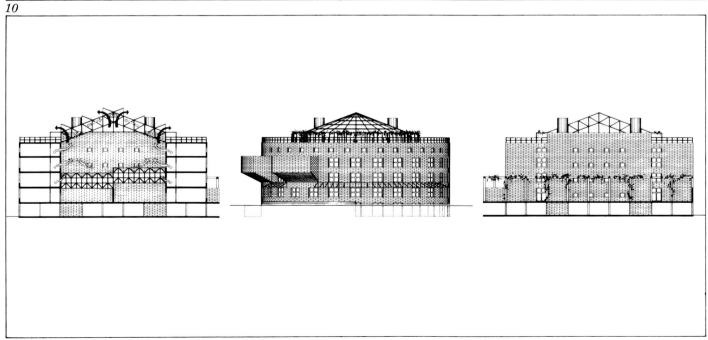
11

Carlsburg Hochschule

12 Northeast elevation.
13 Southwest elevation.
14 Facade section.

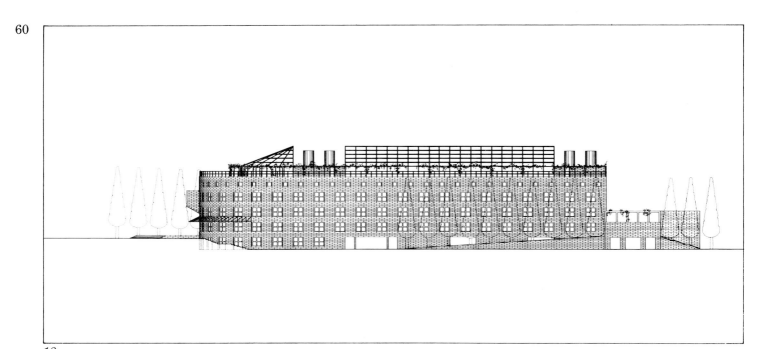
12

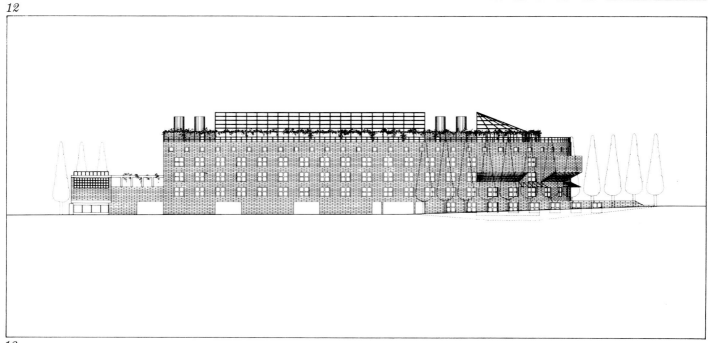
13

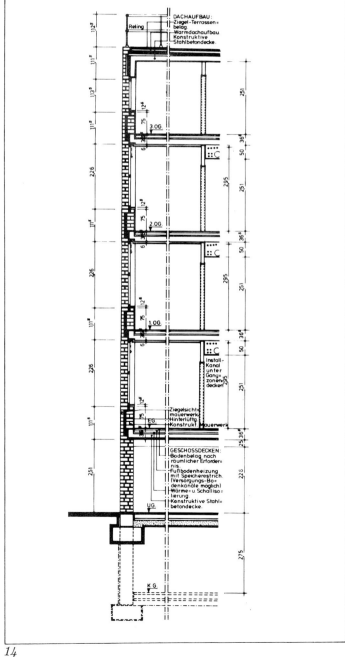

3. by driving the air upward and causing a vacuum through a suction apparatus incorporated into the heat recovery unit on the ridge of the roof, it is possible to create sufficient low pressure in the glazed hall to induce the forced air ventilation of the adjacent volumes;

4. to prevent overheating in the summer, segments of the roof covering can be opened. In this way unwanted heat condensation can be easily drawn off and additional cross-ventilation made possible.

Baden State Library
(In Memory of Friedrich Weinbrenner)

Karlsruhe   1979

Contextual Conception
The existing fabric of a given city must always be allowed to determine the scale and formal language of a specific design. In the case of Karlsruhe, the following were decisive factors:
1. the dominant position of St. Stephan's church within the municipal square;
2. the site intervals indicated by the historical edifices and the structure of the open space;
3. the scale of the surrounding buildings and the predominantly classical character of the architecture;
4. the intended construction of the city according to Weinbrenner's original proposal.

Weinbrenner never thought of the Katholische Stadtkirche as an isolated edifice. In his model, the church had two lateral inner courts which were flanked by four corner structures. Taking Weinbrenner's scheme as a theme, the existing corner building erected on the site after the Second World War should be complemented by three others and the four structures joined by arcades. In this way, the isolated and presently incomprehensible siting of the Ritterstrasse building will be rendered meaningful.

As a parallel to the entrance facade of the church, Weinbrenner's model shows a similarly gabled facade of the same size on the other corner of the side street. In the proposal for the state library, this architectural motif is taken up in a stylistically-adapted form, thereby evoking the historical continuity of the place. The same motif of two opposing buildings with porticoed facades can be found in the market place, which was constructed according to Weinbrenner's plan. Here, the porticoes of the protestant church and the town hall face each other.

The primary urban intention of this project is to complete the block formed by the Erbprinzenstrasse, the Ritterstrasse, the Blumenstrasse and the Herrenstrasse with a continuous-perimeter edifice. The existing constructions on the property will be spatially and architecturally drawn into the proposed reconstruction. The two historical buildings will be preserved and included within the spatial concept as will the existing trees.

The property will be divided into two different segments by the garage entry on the Blumenstrasse: the state library will occupy the eastern segment, and the remaining western half will be occupied by the municipal park and the existing development along the Herrenstrasse. The small scale housing complex on the Herrenstrasse is conceived of as a closed architectural volume. Morphologically speaking, the block will be treated as an excavated architectural volume, thereby providing a diverse sequence of interior courts.

The middle zone of the block will be kept as a green open space, in which certain contingent objects retain their autonomy, including a new gateway structure to be built on the Erbprinzenstrasse as a deliberate historical allusion to the Ettlingen gateway. An existing classical edifice will close this green court on the south, while a central freestanding pergola will frame the garden entrance to the library.

The library itself will be rendered as a geometrically-austere mass surrounding an inner court, which is lined by an arcade—a reference to Weinbrenner's famous Kaiserstrasse arcade. The patio will be treated as a romantic landscape garden, in contrast to the geometric order of the court. In morphological terms, a reciprocal transformation is established between the closed mass-form and the open space-form.

Architectural Conception
The library design is a "decomposition" of the adjacent St. Stephan's church. The architectural forms of the church—nave transept, gable, rotunda, quadrangle, etc.—are resumed and transformed. The church and library compositions employ the same language but in varied form.

The new library is structured so that the areas of major activity—the main card catalogue, the bibliographic reference room, the reading room, and the periodicals section—are all accessible from the main hall. Adjoining the main card catalogue is the catalogue division, also located on the ground floor. The new acquisitions section is on the first floor and is connected to the magazine section. The department of library science, located in the basement, is illuminated by a light shaft. The main reading room, centrally

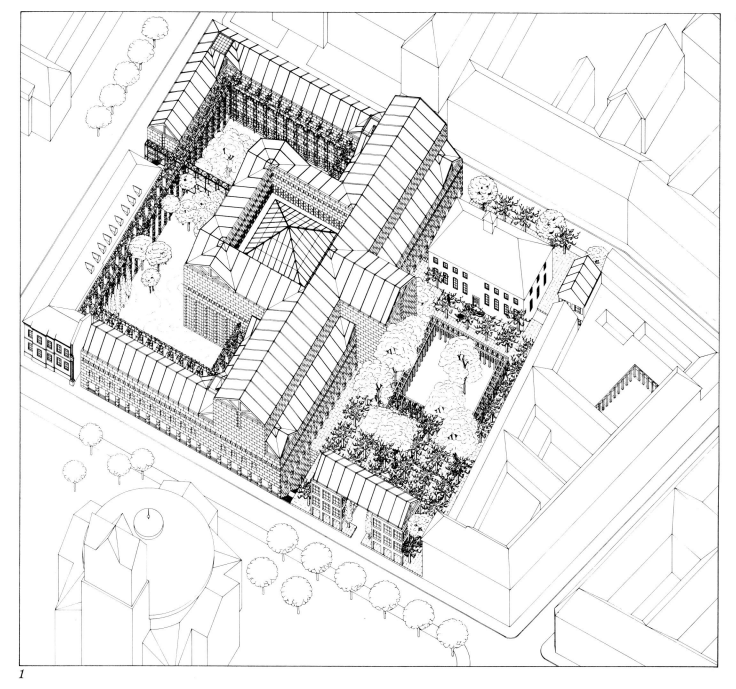

1 Baden State Library, Karlsruhe, 1979. Axonometric.

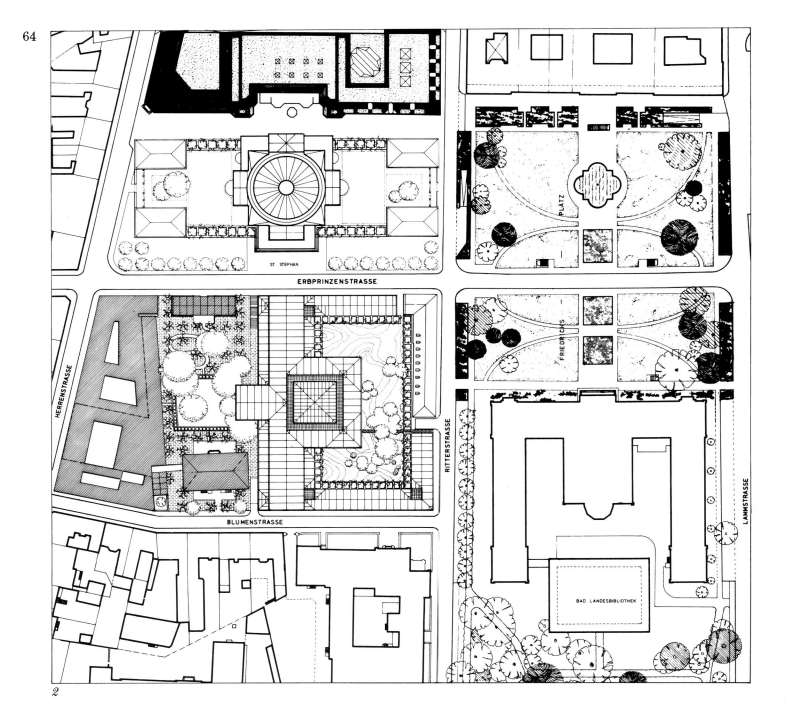

Baden State Library

2 Site plan.
3 Ground floor plan.
4 First floor plan.

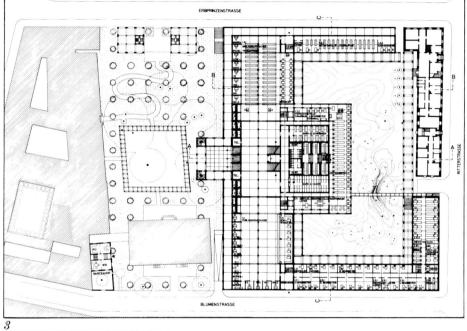

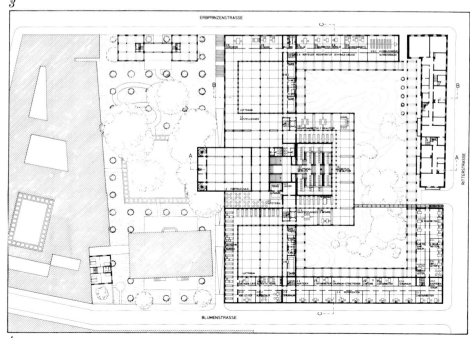

Baden State Library

5 Second floor plan.
6 Fourth floor plan.
7 Section A-A.
8 Section B-B.

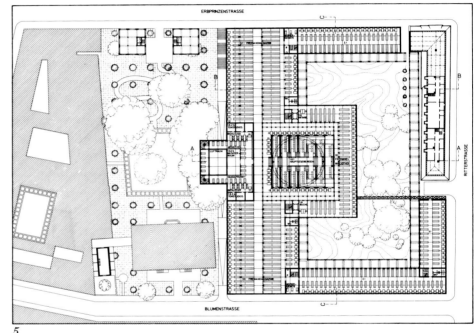

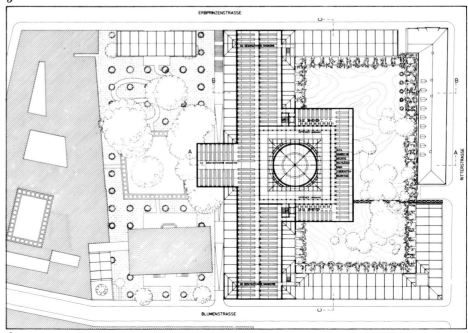

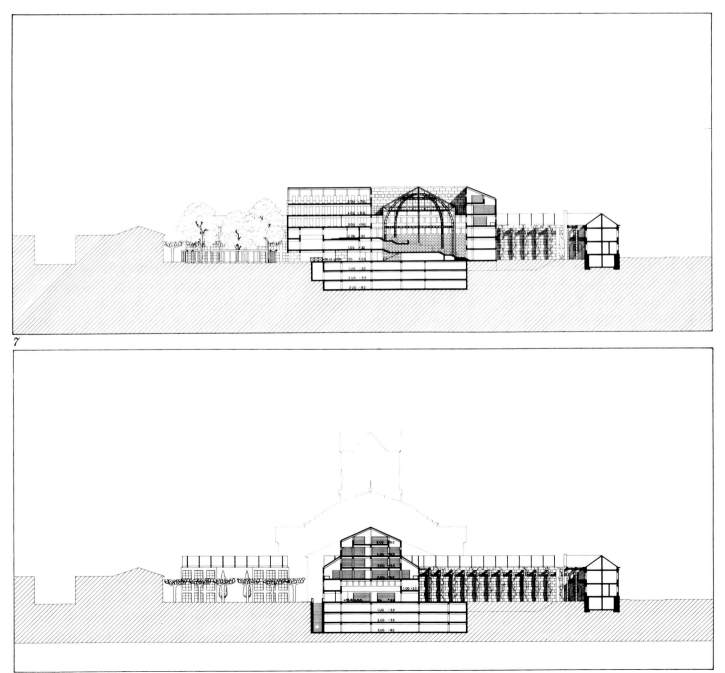

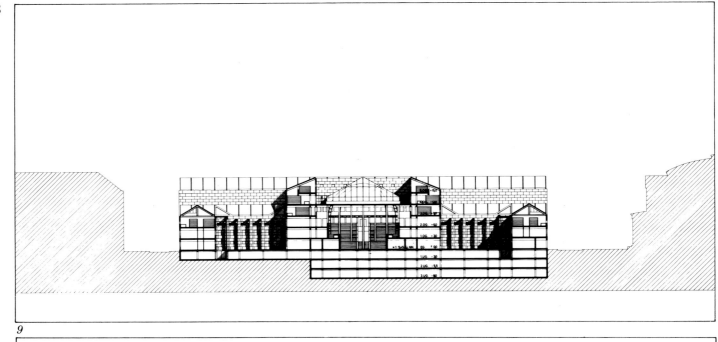

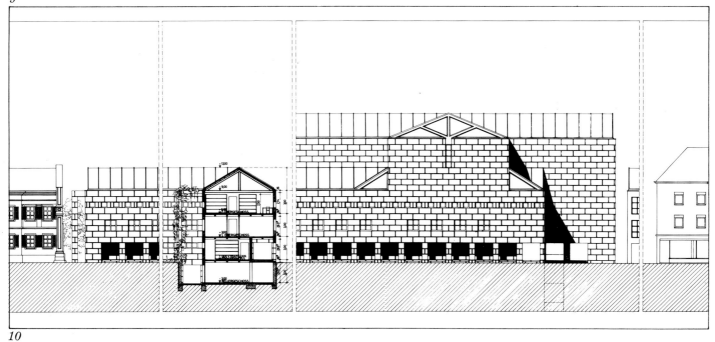

Baden State Library

9 Section C-C.
10 Facade evolvement.
11 Blumenstrasse elevation.
12 Erbprinzenstrasse elevation.

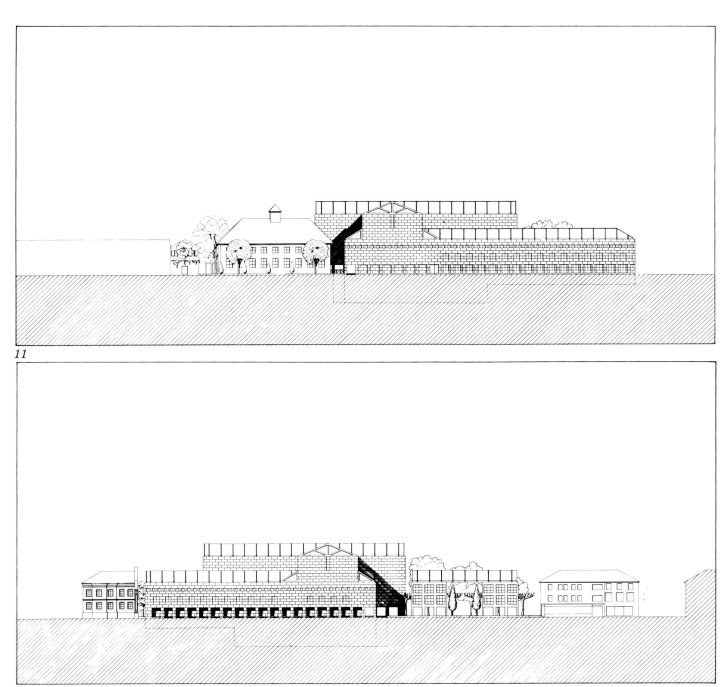

placed, functions as a distributor to the special reading rooms which surround it, and which look over the quiet, inner court. Should it ever become necessary, the high arcade could be glazed and used as an additional reading area.

The main reading room is treated as a stepped volume and covered by a glass cupola. An auxiliary lecture hall opens off the first floor surrounding this central volume. Adjacent cafeteria and mezzanine exhibition space overlook the two-story volume of the bibliographic reference room.

The periodicals section is situated on the second and third floors, while the fourth and fifth floors are given over to closed stacks.

Three levels of underground parking are provided beneath the main building holding 203 automobiles and by extension into a second basement this number could be easily increased to 277.

The main bulk of the library is conceived of as a concrete and masonry construction. The exterior is to be rendered i smooth plaster into which a design simulating the classical bonding of masonry may be etched, thereby continuing the classical urban tradition of Karlsruhe. For a similar reason the roof surface is to be covered with copper and articulated with pediments and mono–pitches. This vocabulary is consciously traditional and is derived from historical sources.

13

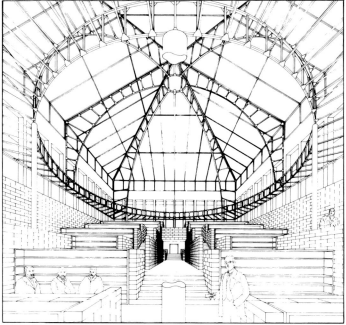
14

Baden State Library

13 Main reading room (with Weinbrenner and assistants).
14 Main reading room. Perspective.
15 Foyer.
16 Inner courtyard.
17 Entry hall.
18 Gatehouse.

Rebuilding the Lützowplatz

Berlin 1980

Before the Second World War a visual axis ran along the diagonal of the rectangular Lützowplatz. After the devastations of the war, however, the existence of the square was completely ignored by traffic engineers and planners who set about building a thoroughly over-scaled traffic intersection. Except for a few remaining structures along the eastern side of the original square, the former boundaries have disappeared.

This proposed rebuilding of a city block along the Landgrafenstrasse is predicated on two assumptions: first, that the square's western wall should be reconstructed, albeit in a somewhat altered position, and second, that gaps in the row of existing structures on the city block side should be filled.

The buildings facing the square create a closed wall and due to a noise ordinance, none of the living quarters of the apartments faces out onto the square, but instead face west toward the quiet interior of the block. Both the south and north sides of the block are unsuitable for the location of apartments. The urban context on the Landgrafenstrasse is restrictive due to the overshadowing from high-rise buildings. The situation on the Lützowplatz is potentially preferable, although it is adversely influenced by its northern orientation. Therefore, the existing structures have been extended into terraces, with the apartments facing east.

Access to the block's interior is via an access road and a pedestrian walk, the latter doubling as a playground. This road also provides access to the underground garage and to the Parkstrasse. Four free-standing houses with four apartments in each are accessible from this point. It is also possible to reach the ground floor apartments from the pedestrian walk.

Although the project aims at a closure of the block perimeter, it also attempts to individuate the separate dwelling elements. Thus, while it is essential that a wall-like construction be erected facing the Lützowplatz, if any residual aspect of the old city square is to be recognized, a strong differentiation among the structures is equally necessary in order to facilitate their individual construction.

The theme of the design is just that—the creation of a contrast between the public square space and the semi-public and private space within the block's interior.

This project addresses the prototypical problems of providing residential space on a main thoroughfare. Thus, both the exigency of the traffic and the requirements of the private domain had to be taken into account. Intimacy and the public domain should be able to co-exist.

The proposal seeks to contrast the idyl of the center of the block with the anonymity of the thoroughfare. The determining factors of the design are closed and open constructions in coexistence with one another. This accounts for the continuous, closed wall that virtually surrounds the block like a skin, forming a public facade, while identifiable separate structures on the reverse side differentiate the interior block space.

*1 Lutzowplatz, Berlin, 1980.
Axonometric.*

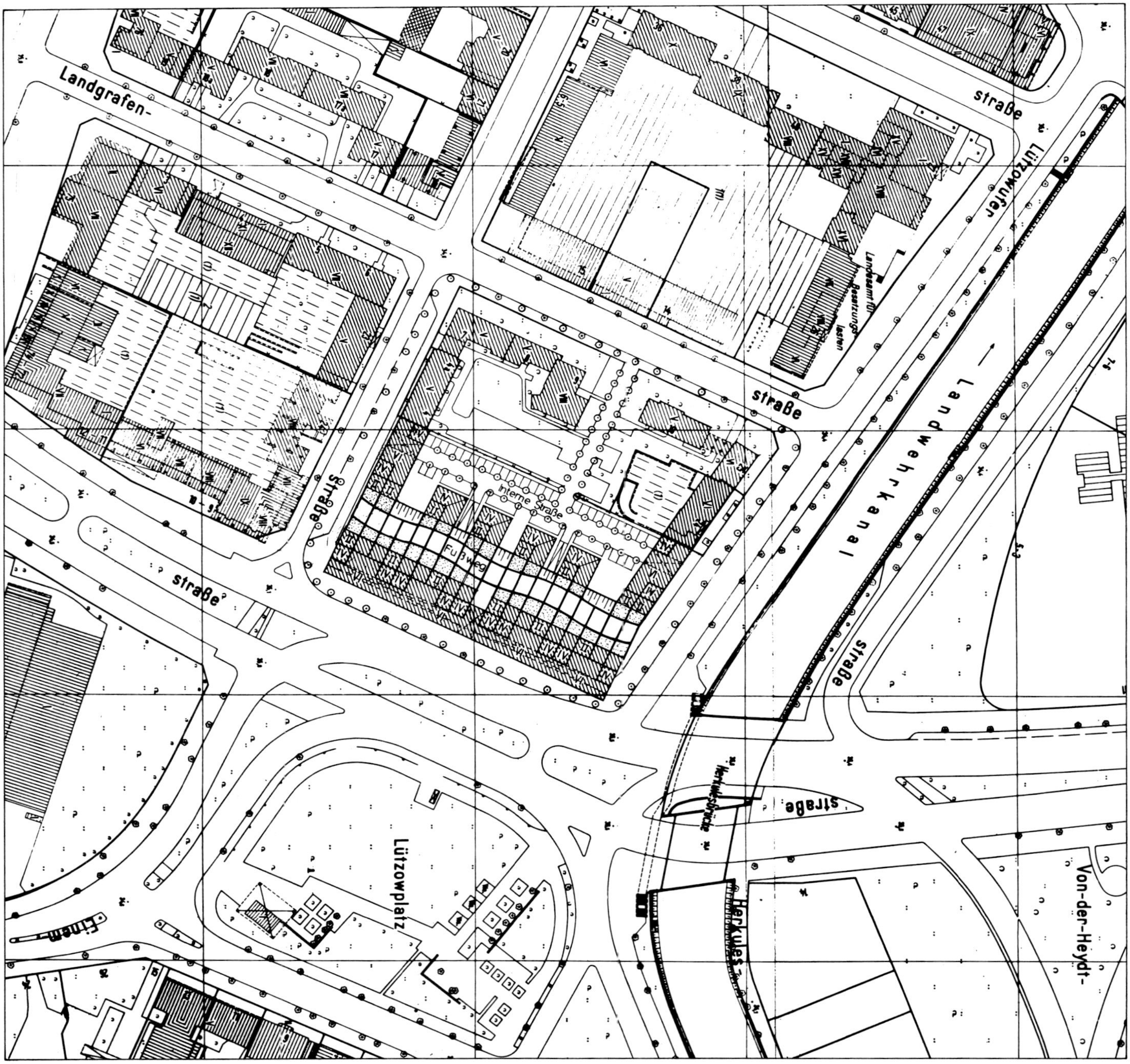
Landgrafen-
straße
Straße
straße
Lützowufer
straße
Landwehrkanal
straße
Interne Straße
Fußweg
Lützowplatz
Herkulesbrücke
straße
Herkules-
Von-der-Heydt-
Einem

2

Lutzowplatz

2 Site plan.
3 Basement plan.

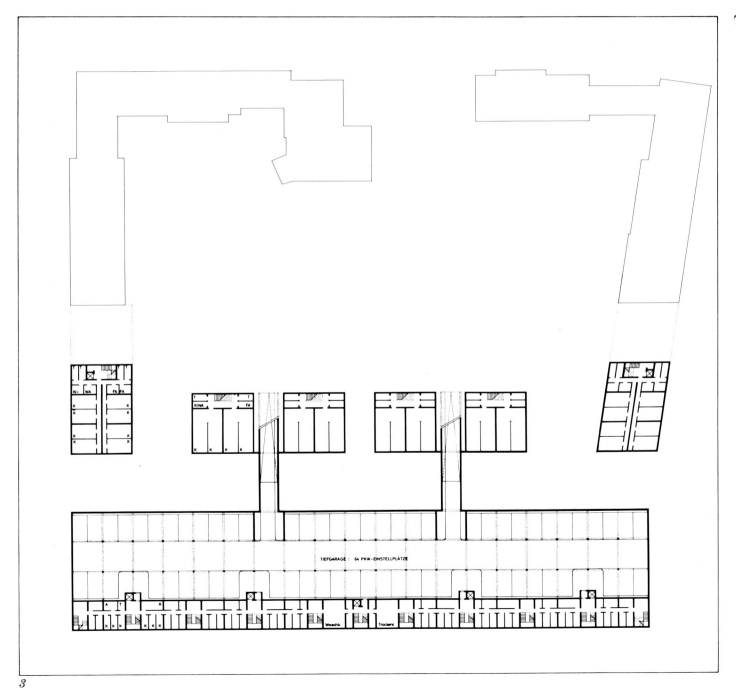

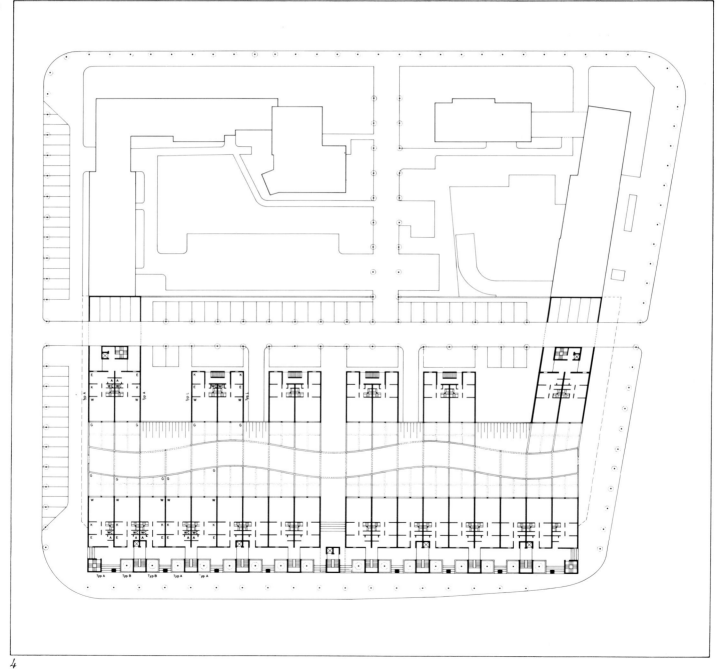

Lutzowplatz

4 Ground floor plan.
5 First floor plan.

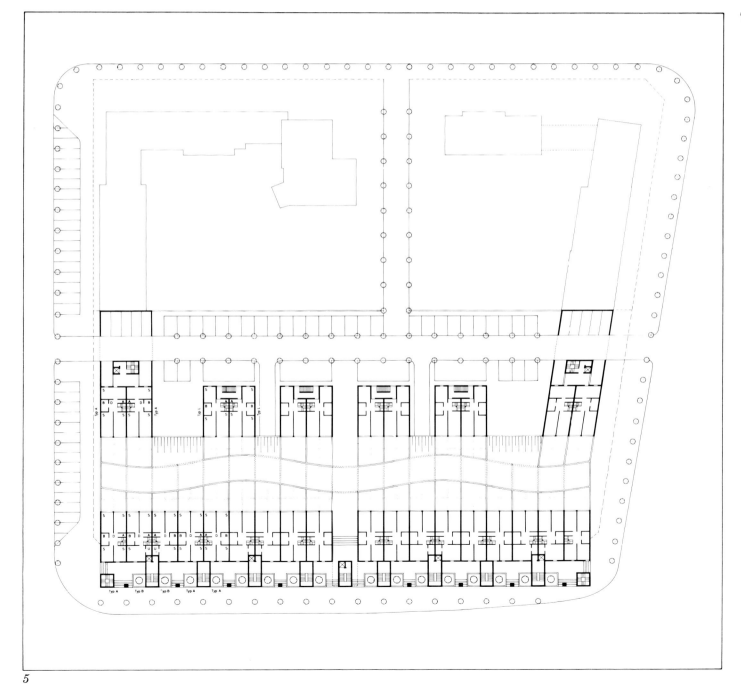

78

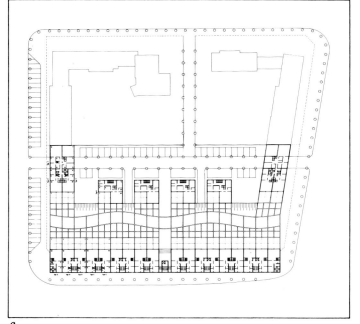

6

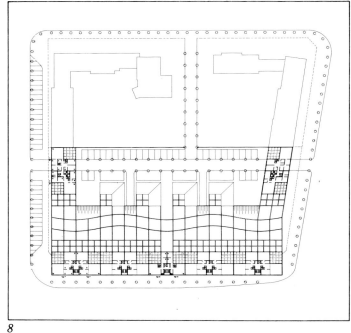

8

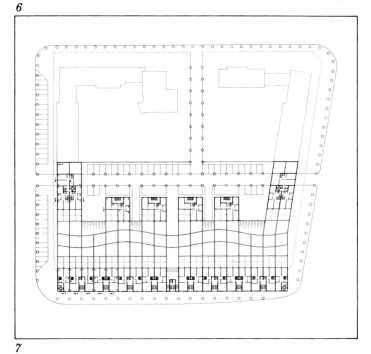

7

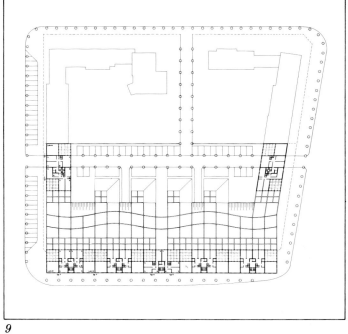

9

Lutzowplatz

6 Second floor plan.
7 Third floor plan.
8 Fourth floor plan.
9 Fifth floor plan.
10 Lutzowplatz elevation.
11 Wichmannstrasse elevation.
12 Section.

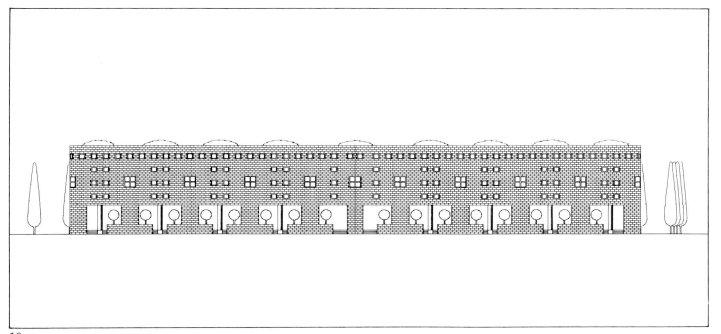

10

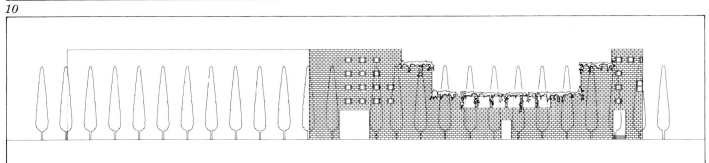

11

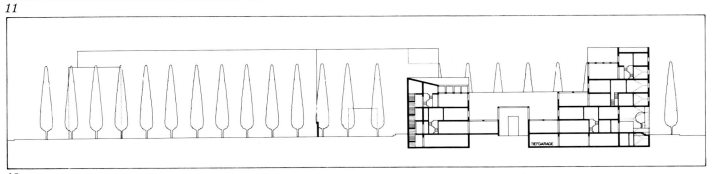

12

Ideas Competition

Ackerhof-Braunschweig   1980

The main difficulty in developing this site along the Georg-Eckert-Strasse lies in the fact that this tract of land is a left-over product from a series of planning measures carried out during the last few years. These measures were of such a diverse nature that developing a unified building project out of the various contexts which had been haphazardly developed in the surrounding area was virtually impossible.

The urban elements which now influence this particular district include, on the one hand, everything from a department store that is completely disproportionate and at variance with the context, to, on the other hand, the intimate scale of the half-timbered buildings along the Langedammstrasse or the medieval structures in the sector around the Magnikirche.

In addition, a number of individual, late-classical buildings are interesting not only for their urban quality but also for their architectonic stature. The Magnikirche dominates the central area of these building clusters and imparts a certain identity and a sense of historical permanence to the surroundings.

The traffic flow projected for the Georg-Eckert-Strasse has a considerable influence on the site, since it will not only separate the building area from the Schlosspark, but it is also completely out of scale with the delicate network of existing streets.

In terms of urban planning, the site is unquestionably redolent of conflict. The point of departure and goal of the proposed design is, therefore, to overcome this difficulty through architectural and urban transformations.

Along the Langedammstrasse, the proposal takes the form of converting existing structures into single-family units. At the same time a cluster of urban villas or *Stadtvillen* is projected as a revival of a type which was once prevalent in Bruanschweig, especially in the Grünring along the Ockergraben. Due to urban, architectonic, economic and social considerations, the urban villa offers essential advantages over the more common row house or multistory apartment dwelling.

The design of a number of individual houses suggested the creation of a public space or square together with a small garden. The square is in this instance, animated by a wide stairway which also doubles as an open-air theater. The historical components used in the design of this square are intended to engender an *Ort der Erinnerung* or "place of recollection." At the southern end of the square a gateway building is shown spanning the space between the structures on either side. At the same time, this square will be connected to the Schlosspark by a pedestrian bridge. The overwhelming mass of the department store will be mitigated by a multistory building that is gradually stepped down to the scale of a series of more modestly proportioned structures.

The other two urban villas contain apartments of different sizes which are designed to echo the architectonic texture of the surroundings.

The area to the east of Ackerhof is dominated by medieval *Zeile* or row houses along a street known as Hinter der Mangikirche ("behind the Magnikirche"). The proposal takes up the irregular form of these *Zeile* in an inflected way and thus creates an enclosure on the park side of the site. Simultaneously, the project respects the particularly small scale of the medieval fabric as well as the larger urban context of the new traffic artery and the Schlosspark. The individual houses, conceived of as urban dwellings, create a continuous arcade facing the park. At the same time they provide apartments with enclosed courts facing the quiet enclosure to the south. On the ground floor, these houses are accessible from a service street equipped with individual garages.

The overall architectural concept finds its complement in the surrounding landscape design of lawns, avenues, groves, freestanding trees, facades ornamented with vines, pergolas, and terraces.

The total plan provides for 36 apartments, 18 single-family houses, 18 garages, 48 parking spaces, and about two square meters of commercial space.

1 Ideas Competition, Ackerhof-Braunschweig, 1980. Site axonometric.
2 House Type 3. South elevation.
3 Section A-A.
4 First level plan.

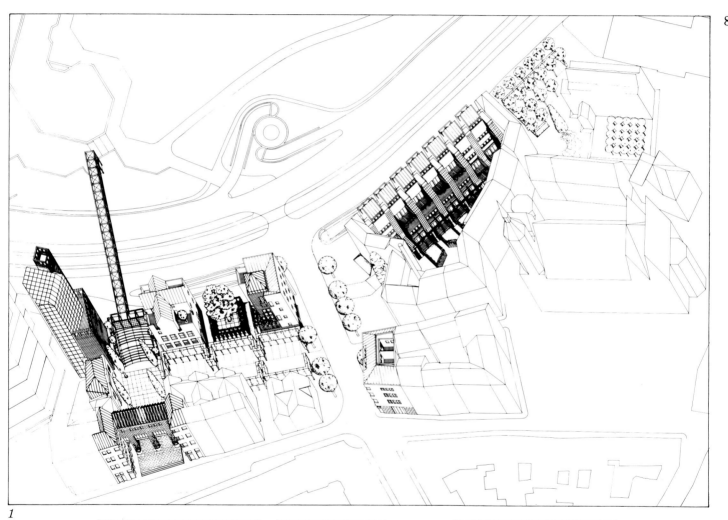

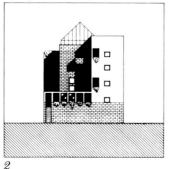

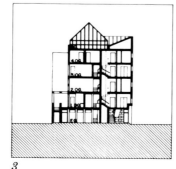

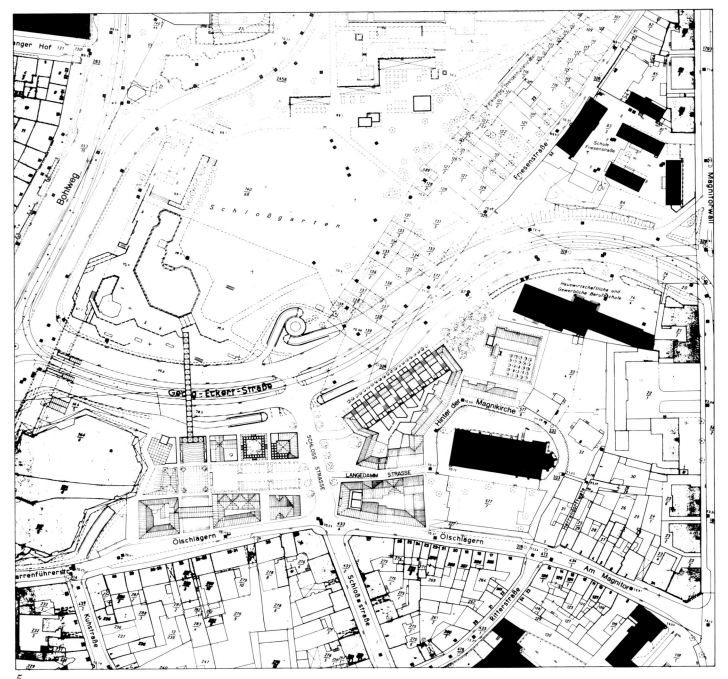

Ideas Competition

5 Site plan.
6 Site plan. One-family housing, with additional living quarters.
7 North elevation.
8 Section A-A.
9 Section B-B.

84

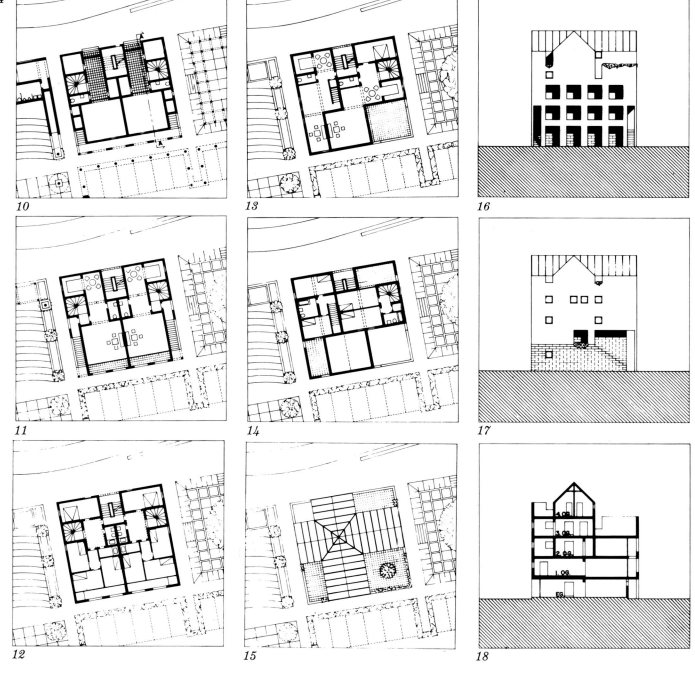

Ideas Competition

10 House Type 2. Ground floor plan.
11 First floor plan.
12 Second floor plan.
13 Third floor plan.
14 Fourth floor plan.
15 Roof plan.
16 South elevation.
17 West elevation.
18 Braunschweig. Section A-A.
19 House Type 1. Ground floor plan.
20 First floor plan.
21 Second and third floor plan.
22 Fourth floor plan.
23 Fifth-eighth floor plan.
24 Section A-A.
25 South elevation.

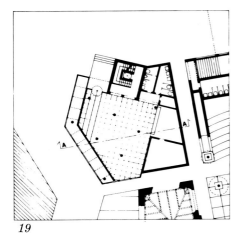
19

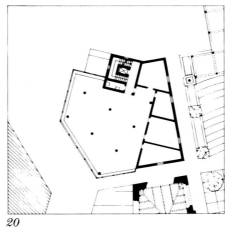
20

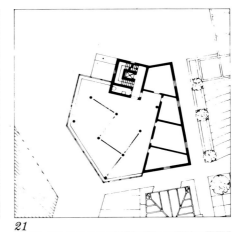
21

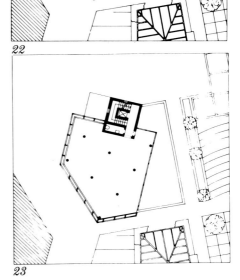
22

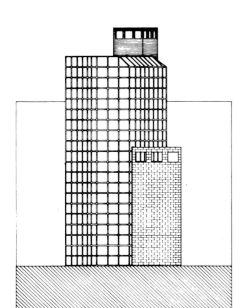
25

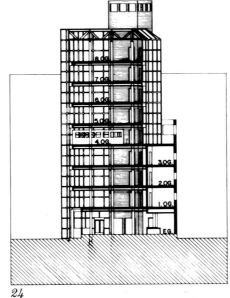
24

23

Marktplatz Competition

Hildesheim   1980

In the context of their historical development, square and loggia are two elements that belong close together and complement each other. The municipal loggia probably fell victim to unimaginative city planners who made functional rather than spatial organization their main criterion. In place of the passageways, arcades, and loggias that historically were planned as public spaces, there arose the unfortunate substitute of dividing the city into pedestrian and functional zones. With regard to the urban open space left by history, a unique opportunity presents itself in the city of Hildesheim to take up again a historic tradition of the spatial arrangement of urban free-spaces and to continue that tradition in a historical sense.

The marketplace at Hildesheim is a street-square, formed by two parallel streets and dominated by the city hall. The intention is to reduce the marketplace to its original size and scale by introducing new buildings on the northern side.

The center of Hildesheim has been traditionally structured by freestanding objects. The primary intervention here is the provision of a multiuse urban loggia modeled along the lines of Andrea Palladio's basilica in Vicenza. The projected loggia comprises a large two story hall with a massive wooden roof, surrounded by an arcade made out of "hollow" brick piers. Open stairways connect the two levels of the loggia to the garage below. The overall plan has been kept as simple as possible so as to accommodate many different kinds of activities.

A bridge linking the loggia to the new city hall permits its upper levels to be used as municipal offices, while the lower level may be used for marketing activities of all kinds as well as for art exhibitions, theatrical performances, concerts, local festivals, balls, parties, etc. Above all, the hall is designed to be a meeting place, and with the installation of glass doors around the perimeter, it could be easily utilized throughout the year.

The most difficult decision facing the architect was what to do with the Hotel Rose which is executed in the typically indifferent style of the 1950s. The final proposal was to cover the facade with a trellis of plants. This combined with a planted arcade would soften the general ambience of the square.

The front edge of the municipal loggia is approximately aligned with the historical fabric. The edge of the roof as well as the building structure are taken from the historical context. The outer masonry structure of the loggia forms a ring which supports a large wooden roof. A three-gabled *non-historicist* facade vaguely profiled after the traditional pattern caps the main facade to the marketplace.

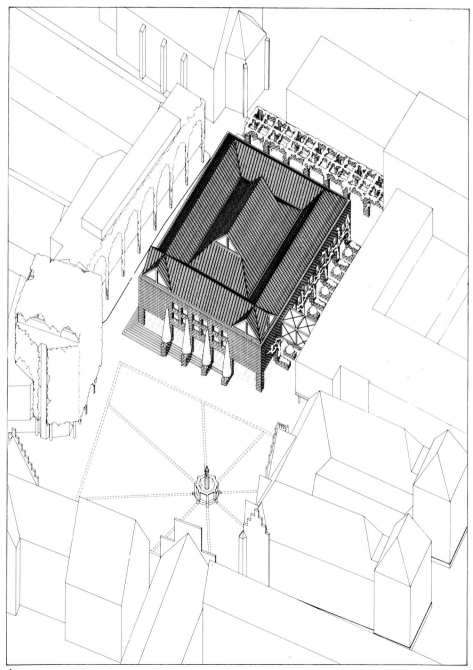

1 Marktplatz Competition, Hildesheim, 1980. Site axonometric.

Hildesheim

2 Market Place/Street Place.
3 Separate objects.
4 Square in the square.
5 Extension of the square.
6 Square widening.
7 Squares and objects.

8 900.
9 1089.
10 1160.
11 1250.
12 ca. 1600.
13 1653.

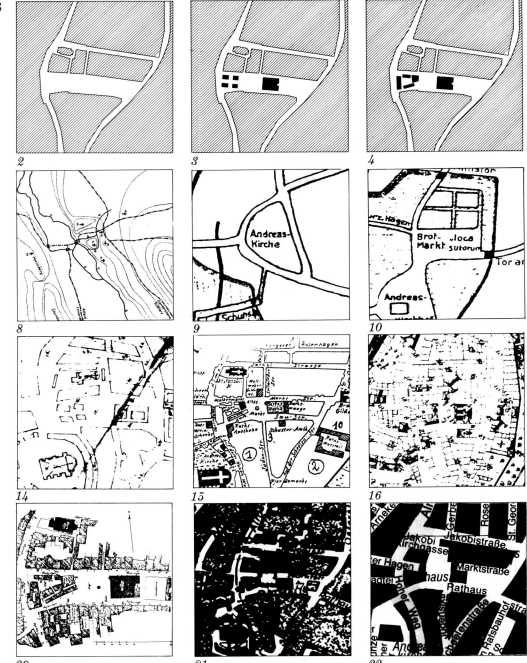

14 1729.
15 1769.
16 1769-1774.
17 1840.
18 1875-1884
19 1890.
20 ca. 1900.
21 1943.
22 1967.
23 1968.
24 1980.
25 1981.

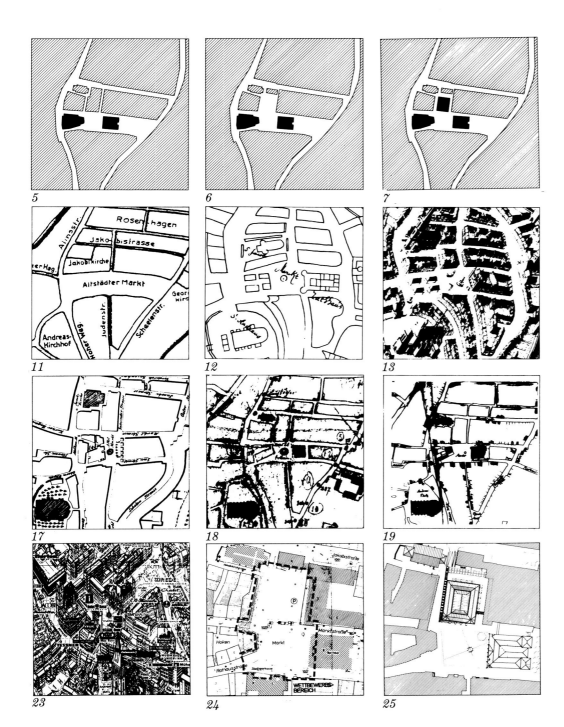

90

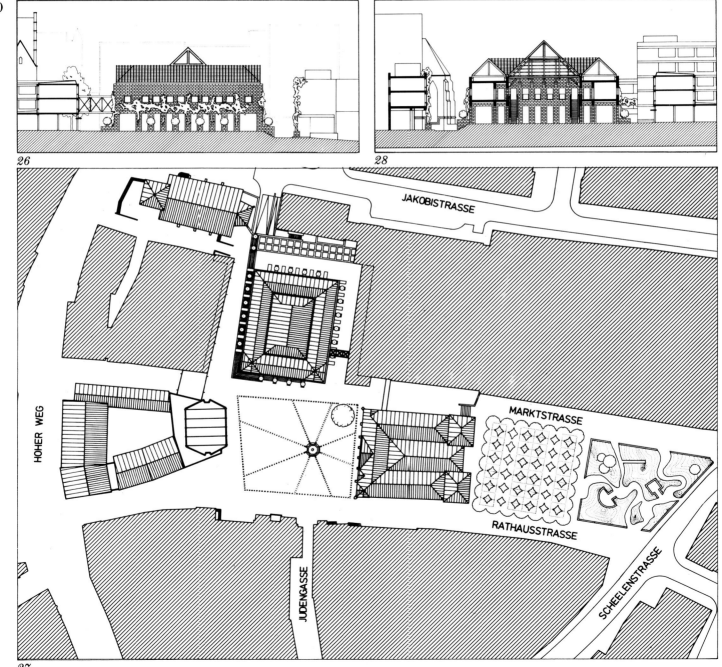

26

28

27

JAKOBISTRASSE
HOHER WEG
MARKTSTRASSE
RATHAUSSTRASSE
JUDENGASSE
SCHEELENSTRASSE

Hildesheim

26 Rear view.
27 Site plan.
28 Section A-A.
29 Secion B-B.
30 Ground floor plan.
31 Section C-C.
32 First floor plan.

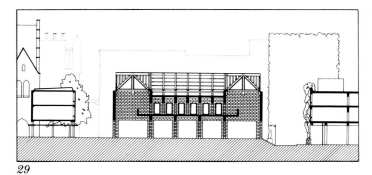
29

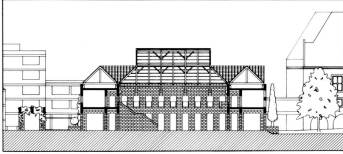
31

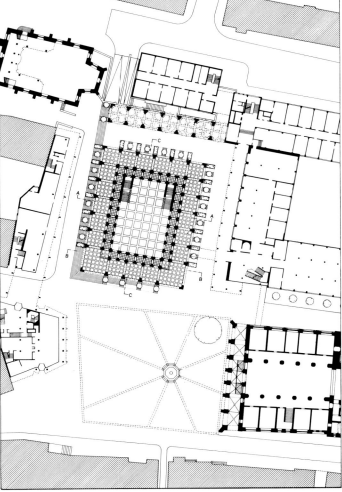
30

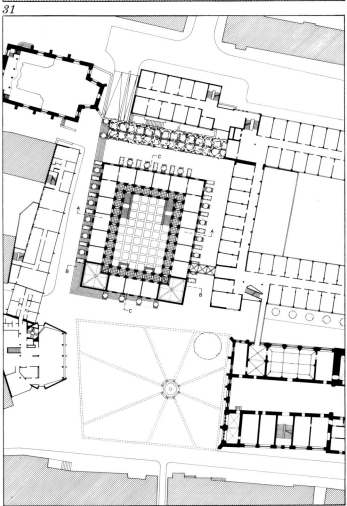
32

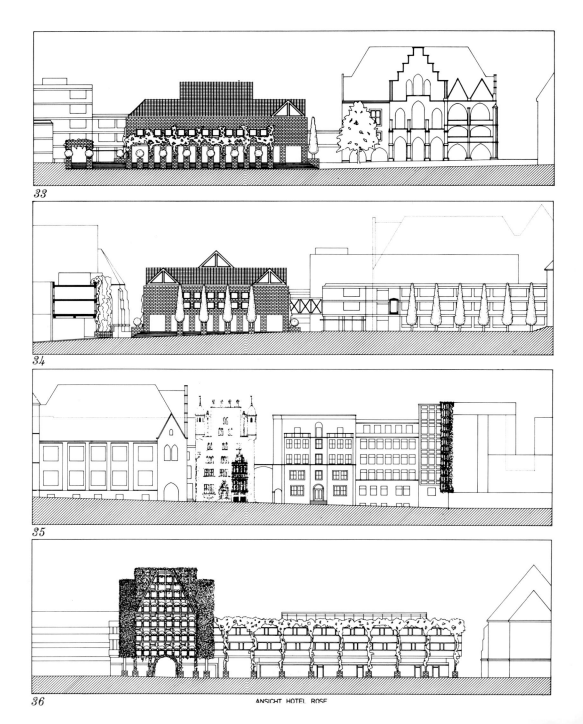

33

34

35

36 ANSICHT HOTEL ROSE

Hildesheim

33 Side elevation.
34 Markstrasse elevation.
35 Rathausstrasse elevation.
36 Hotel Rose elevation.
37 Markplatz proposal. Perspective.
38 Markplatz before 1945.
39 Interior perspective of main hall.
40 Former Rathaus hall. Perspective.

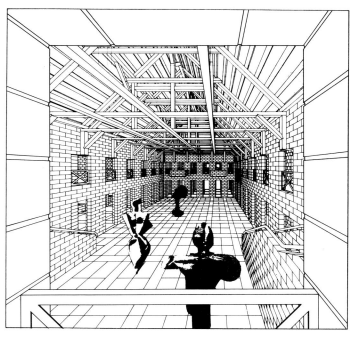

Konstantinplatz

Trier 1981

The Roman basilica which still dominates the Konstantinplatz (Constantine Square) in Trier has a history of remarkable survival. While today the basilica is preceived as a freestanding hall, this hardly corresponds to its original state, when it was flanked by colonnaded courtyards to the east and west of its mass. The Laurentian church which was added to the basilica in the Gothic period was totally demolished by Napoleon in 1803, although throughout the nineteenth century it was encumbered with additional courtyards and palatial structures. In the middle of the century its historical form was restored and it was consecrated as a church on September 28th, 1856. The area around the basilica hardly changed at all between its reconstruction in the mid-nineteenth century and its destruction in the Second World War.

The most impressive setting of the basilica when it was first restored in the nineteenth century was its slightly sunken placement to one side of the precisely cobbled Konstantinplatz. It would obviously be desirable today to come as close as possible to the magnificent austerity of this setting. The area around the basilica was completely razed during the Second World War and the restoration which followed was decidedly unsympathetic to a monument of this stature. The area to the west of the basilica is now being used as a parking lot and the formerly clear spatial integration of the square and the street has patently been lost, leaving an unformed empty space in the center of the city.

Even if one disregards the present destruction of the square by parked cars, the general lack of character of the surroundings is quite astonishing. At the present time, the square looks like a huge backyard, despite the presence of historical structures to the north. Three-story buildings establish the character of the square at the western edge, along a broken frontage where the square loses its definition as it opens towards the Konstantinstrasse. The eastern end of the square is completed with its Renaissance gate and Baroque tower.

Ungers's proposal for the central area of the historic core of Trier is set within the present overall planning provision for the city. A ring boulevard diverts most of the through traffic away from the central area, while at the same time giving access to underground garages located near the center, which are intended to facilitate access to the core of the city. This specific proposal would complement the above strategy in the following way: the area bordered by Sudallee, Weberbach and Mustorstrasse is characterized by the parkscape of the palace garden where, apart from the western edge of the site, most of the structures are large-scale, solitary buildings. This includes the remains of the medieval city wall and the ruins of the Imperial Baths. On the whole, this neighborhood fulfills the function of an inner-city recreation area, and the residential quarters of the inner city should be linked to the park as closely as possible. The present pedestrian route to the park is via the Konstantinplatz, so that the lowering of the square should be limited to a few sections. The connection between the square and the park is via a path on the same level and a ramp rising out of the lower area of the square. The continuation of this ramp as an avenue establishes the western edge of the part; in doing so it not only unites heterogeneous buildings but also creates a visual link between the Imperial Baths and the Konstantinplatz.

Six trial proposals were made for the Konstantinplatz before the development of this final proposal, which in some ways may be regarded as the reconstruction of an archaeological memory. The component parts of the present proposal are the following:
1. the lowering of the entrance area of the basilica to the level of the Roman city and the spatial reconstruction of the entrance court;
2. the construction of an arcade structure or urban loggia in order to close off the bordering buildings;
3. the construction of a tower on the foundations of the Laurentian parish church;
4. the reconstruction of the entrance portico by means of negative forms;
5. the construction of a square sunken area in front of the portico structure;
6. the provision of a gate building to close off the Konstantinstrasse;
7. the recreation of the planting pattern in front of the former administrative building.

1 Konstantinplatz, Trier, 1981.
Original site axonometric.

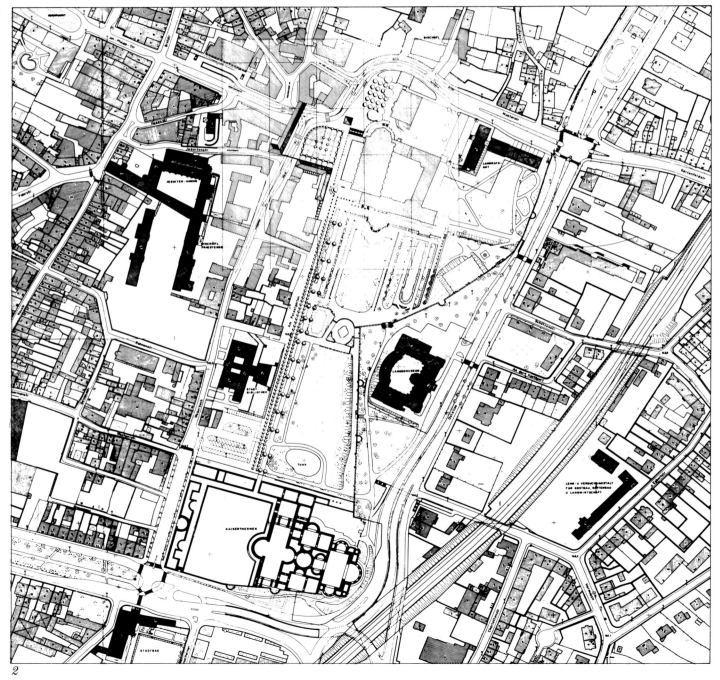

Konstantinplatz

2 Site plan.
3 Block plan.

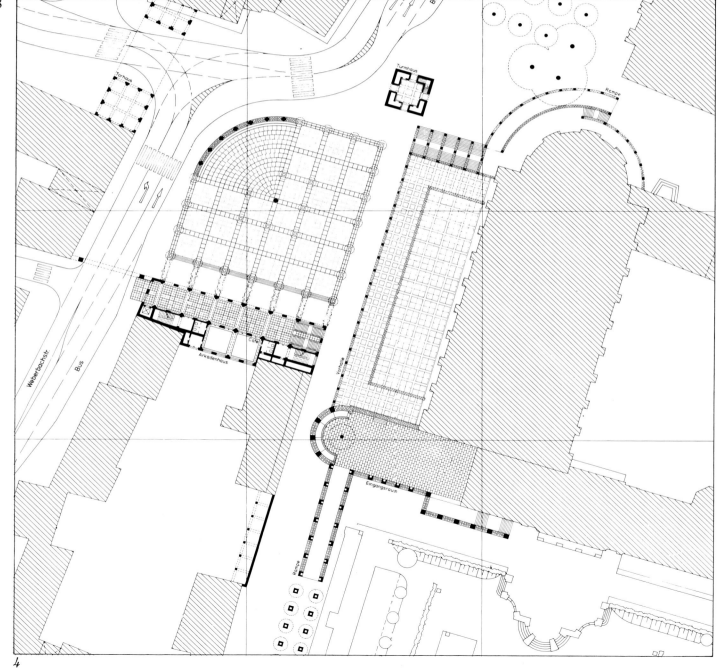

Konstantinplatz

4 Second level plan.
5 Third level plan.

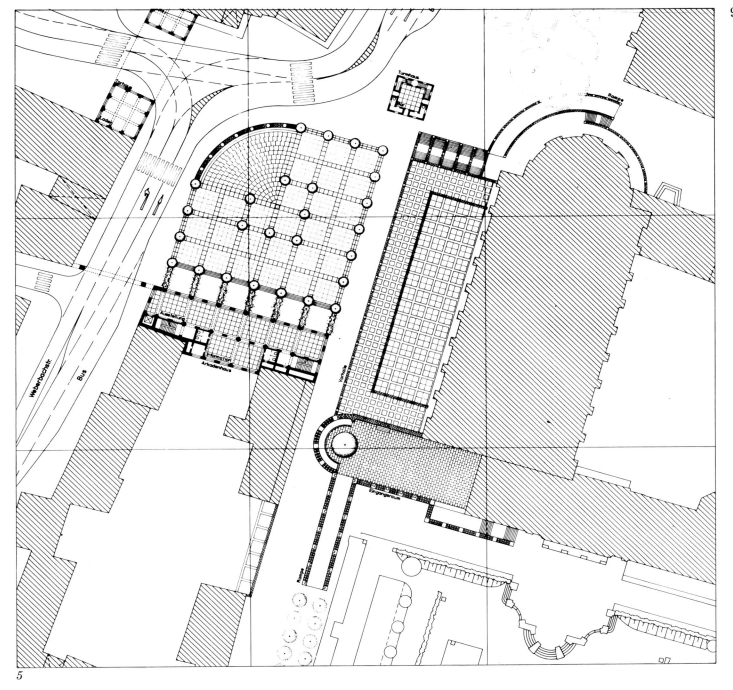

100

6

Konstantinplatz

6 Fourth level plan.
7 Site axonometric.

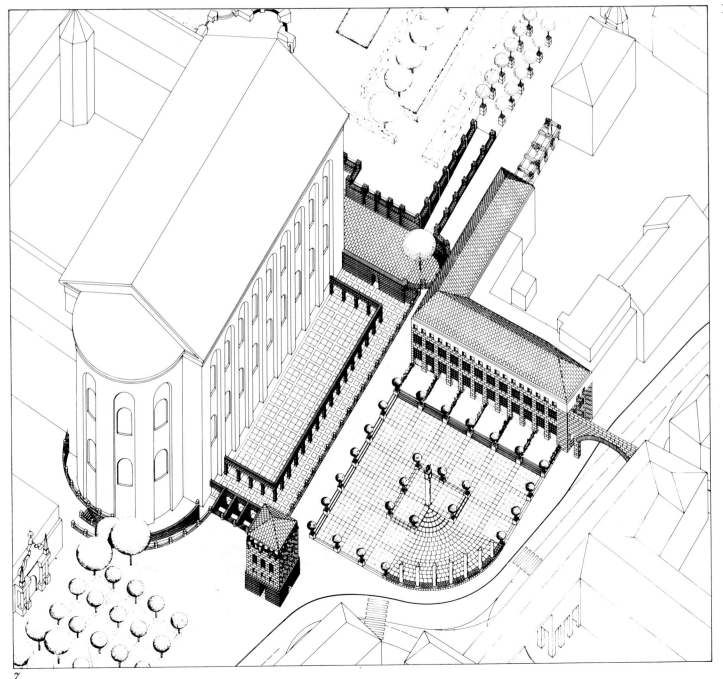

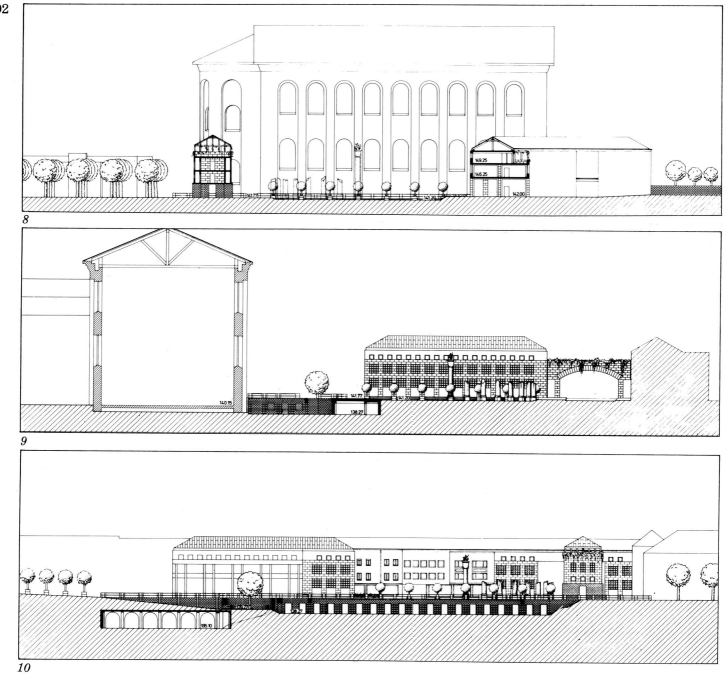

Konstantinplatz

8 West section and elevation.
9 North section and elevation.
10 East section and elevation.
11 Perspective.

Selected Bibliography

Compiled by Gerardo Brown-Manrique

1953
Schell, Rainer. "Arbeten junger Architekten." *Baukunst Und Werkform* vol.VI, no.8, pp.386,409-414.

1954
"Hans in Koln." *Bunkunst Und Werkform* vol.VIII, no.7/8 pp.415-421.
"Quelques Examples d'Equipement le Sejour." *L'Architecture d'Aujourd'hui* vol.25, no.56 (September/October), pp.38-39, 53, 81.

1955
"Huis voor bejaard echtpaar." *BOUW* no.9 (26 February), p.183.
"Entwurf fur den Neubau des 'Oberhausener Instituts'." *Baukunst und Werkform* vol.VIII, no.3, pp.142, 153-161.

1956
Hoffmann, Ot, and Christoph Repenthin. *Neue Urbane Wohnformen—Gartenhofhauser, Tereichsiedlungen, Terrassenhauser* (Berlin: Verlag Ullstein GmbH), p.91.
"Ein Wohnhause in Koln." *Die Kunst Und Das Schone Heim* vol.54, no.5 (February), pp.192-195.
"Kleines Wohnhaus Rodenkirchen bei Koln." *Baukunst und Werkform* vol.IX, no.5. pp.260-262.

1957
"Instituto Preparatorio de Estudos Universitadios, Oberhausen, Alemania." *Habibat—Arquitetura e Artes do Brasil* no.44 (September), pp.8-9.

1958
"Interessante Bungalow—Bauten—diese Konnte ein Haus der Zukunftsein." *Die Wolksheimstatte* vol.10, no.11 (November), p.16
Mittag, Martin, ed. *Kleinsthauser—Ferienhauser—Bungalows* (Gutersloh: C. Bertelsmann Verlag), p.59.

1959
Wolff, Rainer. *Das Klein Haus* (Munich: Verlag Georg D.W. Callwey), pp.54-55.
"Ein idealer Grundiss." *Die Volksheimstatte* vol.11, no.5 (May), p.6.
"Internat des Staatlichen Instituts zur Erlangung der Hochschulreife, Oberhausen." *Bauwelt* vol.50, no.51/52 (December), pp.1506-1509.
"Studentenheim in Koln-Lindenthal." *Bauwelt* vol.50, no.51/52 (21 December), pp.1516-1518.

1960
"Ein Werkstattbricht—Bauten und Projekten von O.M. Ungers." *Bauwelt* vol.51, no.8 (22 February), pp.204-217.
Rossi, Aldo. "Un giovane architetto tedesco: Oswald Mathias Ungers." *Casabella* no.244 (October), pp.22-35.
"O. Mathias Ungers—the Architect's Own House, Cologne-Mungersdorf." *Architectural Design* vol.30, no.11 (November), pp.455-457.

1961
"Wir bauen eine Garage mit Kunsthalle...aus dem Programm des Landesbauwettbewerbs Kunsthalle Dusseldorf." *Bauwelt* vol.52, no.1 (2 January), pp.14-17.
Ungers, O.M. "Fur eine lebendige Baukunst...." *Bauwelt* vol.52, no.8 (20 February), pp.193, 196.
"Wohnhaus in Rodenkirchen bei Koln." *Deutsche Bauzeitschrift* no.2, pp.153-154.
"Institut d'Einseignement Oberhausen, Allemagne." *L'Architecture d'Aujourd'hui* vol.32, no.94 (February/March), pp.14-15.
"New German Schools." *Architectural Review* vol.130, no.773 (July), pp.8-9.
Ungers, O.M. "Aus einem vortrag vor dem Akademischen Architekten Verein in Hannover." *Baukunst und Werkform* vol.XIV, no.8, p.426.
"Wohnhaus in Koln—Mungersdorf." *Baukunst und Werkform* vol.XIV, no.8, pp.427-428, Technisches Supplement, pp.1-4.
Pevsner, Nikolaus. "Moderne Architektur und der Historiker oder Die Wiederkehr Historizismus." *Deutsche Bauzeitung* vol.66, no.10 (October), pp.757-764.

1962
Conrads, Ulrich, and Marschall, Werner. *Contemporary Architecture in Germany* (New York: Praeger Publishers), pp.9, 39-41, 44. Published in Great Britain as *Modern Architecture in Germany* (London: The Architectural Press); translation of the German edition, *Neue Deutsche Architektur* (Stuttgart: Verlag Gerd Hatje).
Conrads, Ulrich. "Focus VI: O.M. Ungers." *Zodiac* no.9, pp.172-181.
"Berichte—Eine Stimme aus England zu neuen Deutschen Schulen." *Bauwelt* vol.53, no.3 (15 January), pp.77-79.
"Works of O.M. Ungers." *The Kentiku* (March), pp.27-42.
"Wohnhaus in Wuppertal." *Bauwelt* vol.53, no.27 (2 July), pp.768-769.
"Krafte und Gegenkrafte." *Bauwelt* vol.53, no.28/29 (16 July), pp.803-805.
Schmitt, Karl Wilhelm. "Im Schnittpunkt von Kaflinien." *Bauwelt* vol.53, no.28/29 (16 July), pp.793-797, 800-807.

1963
Bundesdeutscher Architekten BDA-Koln. *Sonderdruck aus Bauten Kolner Architekten 1948-1963* (Darmstadt: Verlag das Beispiel, May), pp.62-63, 76-77, 100.
Schwarz, Maria; Rosiny Klaus, Joachim Schurmann and O.M. Ungers, eds. *Rudolf Schwarz* (Heidelberg: F.H. Kerle Verlag).
Gieselmann, Reinhardt, and Ungers, O.M. "Zu einer neuen Architektur." *Der Monat* vol.15, (March), p.96. Translation in English published as "Towards a New Architecture" in Conrads, Ulrich, ed.: *Programmes and Manifestoes on 20th Century Architecture* (Cambridge, Massachusetts: MIT Press, 1970), pp.165-166.
Ungers, O.M. "Gesichtspunkte der Planung im Wohnungsbau." *Die Landschaft* no.3.
"Markisches Viertel." *Bauwelt* vol.54, no.14/15 (15 April), pp.390-393.
"Wohnhaus in Koln." *Bauwelt* vol.54, no.14/15 (15 April), p.403.
Huber, Bendikt. "Architektur des Zufalls." *Werk* vol.50, no.7 (July), pp.264-271.
"Zum Projekt 'Neue Stadt' in Koln." *Werk* vol.50, no.7 (July), pp.281-283.
"O.M. Ungers—la sua abitazione-studio a Colonia-Mungersdorf."

Abitare no.21 (November), pp.38-43.

1964
Bauten Kolner Architeckten 1948-1963 (Cologne: Bundes Deutschen Architekten), pp.62-63, 76-77, 100.
Pehnt, Wolfgang, ed. *Encyclopedia of Modern Architecture* (New York: Harry N. Abrams, Inc.), p.127. Originally published in German (Munich: Dromersche Verlaganstalt).
Ungers, O.M. *Die Erscheinungs Formen des Expressionismus in der Architektur* (Cologne: O.M. Ungers, March).
"Koln Neue Stadt." *Bouwkundig Weekblad* vol.82, no.11 (5 June), p.iv.
"Bekroonde antwerpen voor een huisvestingscomplex voor Studenten op Brienerlo." *Bouwkunding Weekblad* vol.82, no.19 (25 September), pp.234-244.
Ravnikar, Edo. "Architektura, Plastika in Slikarstvo." *Sinteza* (Yugoslavia, October), p.8, ill.22.

1965
Eggeling, F. and Ungers, O.M. ed. *Symposium 1964* Stadtebauliches Entwurfsseminar der Architekturstudenten der Technische Universitat Berlin. (Berlin: Facultat fur Architektur).
Koenig, Giovanni Klaus. *Architettura Tedesca del Secondo Dopoguerra* (Bologna: Cappelli), pp.18, 35, 96-100, pls.46-48.
Wohnen in Neue Sidelungen (Stuttgart: Karl Kramer Verlag, pp.45-46, 130-133.
Funke, Hermann. "Neue Architekturkritik—Schlafturme und Negativraume." *Die Zeit* vol.20, no.6 (12 February), p.9.
Ungers, O.M. "Ein fuhrungsvortrag zum Symposium 'Sanierung der Spandauer Alstadt'." *Der Architekt* vol.XIV, no.9 (September).
"Mehrfamilienhaus in Wuppertal." *Baumeister* vol.62, no.10 (October), pp.1081-1083.
Ungers, O.M. "Wochenaufgebau 1964/65." *Veroffentlichungen zur Architektur* no.1 (Berlin: T.U. Berlin, November).
"Wettbewerb Romanisch-Germanisches Museum, Koln." *Baumeister* vol.62, no.11 (November), pp.1275, 1278.
"I protagonisti dell'architettura contemporanea: O.M. Ungers." *Rassegna Dell'Istituto do Architectura e Urbanistica* vol.1, no.3 (December), pp.64-97.
Ungers, O.M. "Insegnamento sviluppo e ricerca." *Casabella* 300 (December), pp.70-71.

1966
Banham, Reyner. *The New Brutalism—Ethic or Aesthetic?* (New York: Reinhold Publishing Co.), pp.125-126, 144-145.
Jacobus, John. *Twentieth-Century Architecture—The Middle Years 1940-65* (New York: Frederick A. Praeger), p.174, fig.333.
Meryer-Bohe, Olinde and Walter. *Neue Wohnhauser* (Stuttgart: Verlagsanstalt Alexander Koch GmbH), pp.22, 58-60.
Schmitt, Karl Willhelm. *Multistory Housing* (New York: Praeger Publishers), pp.96, 106-108, 180-181. Originally published in German as *Mehrgeschossiger Wohnbau* (Stuttgart: Werlag Gerd Hatje).
Weiss, Erhadt. *Neue Stadtteile—Ruckblick und Ausblick* (Frankfurt am Main: Europaische Verlagsanstalt), vol.4, pp.34-35.
"Markisches Viertel, Berlin." *Deutsche Bauzeitung* vol.71, no.1 (January), pp.13-15.
Bauer, Eugen, and Bacher, Max ed. *Die Hauptschule—Volkschulen,* *Schulzentran* Architektur Wettbewerbe no.45 (Stuttgart: Karl Kramer Verlag, February), pp.26-33.
Ungers, O.M. "Gesichtspunkte der Planung beim Wohnungsbau." *Neue Ladschaft* vol.11, no.4 (April), pp.189-194.
"Wettbewerb Flughafen Berlin-Telel." *Bauwelt* vol.57, no.22 (30 May), p.655.
Bisogli, L. "Germania di oggi: O.M. Ungers." *Casabella* no. 305 (May), pp.36-59.
Ungers, O.M. "Erlauterungen zum Projekt Grunzug-Sud in Koln."
Ungers, O.M., Woods, S. and Wewerka, S., eds. "Team X Treffe in Berlin." *Veroffentlichungen zur Architektur* no.3 (Berlin: T.U. Berlin, June).
Ungers. O.M.; Woods, S; and Wewerka, S., eds. "Team X Treffe in Berlin." *Veroffentlichungen zur Architektur* no.3.
Pahl, Jurgen. "Betrachtungen uber das Schaffen der Architekten O.M. Ungers." *Deutsche Bauzeitung* vol. 71, no.7 (July), pp.585-586.
von Einem, Herbert. "Stuffenwettbewerb fur die Museumsbauten in Berlin—das Ergebuis." *Bauwelt* vol.57, no.34/35 (29 August), pp.980-988, 993-997.
"Wettbewerb Romanisch-Germanishes Museum, Koln." *Baumeister* vol.62, no.11 (November), pp.1275-1278.
Ungers, O.M. (critic). "Schnellstrasse und Gebaude" *Veroffentlichungen zur Architektur* no.4 (Berlin: T.U. Berlin).
_____. "Grossformen im Wohnungsbau." *Veroffentlichungen zur Architecktur* no.5 (Berlin: T.U. Berlin, December).

1967
Borsi, F, and G.K. Konig. *Architettura dell'Espressionismo* (Genova: Vitali e Ghianda), pp.14-53.
Ludmann, Harald, and Joachim Riedel. *Neue Stadt Koln-Chorweiler* (Stuttgart: Karl Kramer Verlag).
Nehls, Werner. "'New Brutalism'—Beginn einer neuen Eopch." *Baumeister* vol.64, no.1 (January), pp.75,85.
"Markisches Viertel, Berlin-Reinickendorf." *Baukunst und Werkform* vol.75, no.2 (February), pp.126-134.
"O.M. Ungers—Sozialer Wohnungsbau 1953-1966." *Baumeister* vol.64, no.557 (May), pp.556-572.
Ungers, O.M. (critic). "Platze und Strassen." *Veroffentlichungen zur Architektur* no.8 (Berlin: T.U. Berlin, June).
Ungers, O.M. "Struktur—Quantitat—Dimension." *BAU* Vienna: no. 6 (June), pp.123-145.
_____. "Gutachten Ruhwald." *Veroffentlichungen zur Architektur* no.9. (Berlin: T.U. Berlin, August).
_____. (critic). "Wohnen Am Park" *Veroffentlichungen zur Architektur* no.10.
_____. (critic). "Stadtebauliche Untersuchung Paderborn." *Veroffentlichungen zur Architektur* no.11 (Berlin: T.U. Berlin).
"Stadtebauliche Gutachten fur 'Ruhwald', Berlin." *Bauwelt* vol.58, no.32/33 (14 August), pp.818-825.
"Concours d'Urbanisme pour le Quartier 'Ruhwald', Berlin 1965." *Aujourd'hui: Arts et Architecture* vol.10, no.57/58, p.84.
Lammert, Peter. "L'Enseignement de l'Architecture en Allemagne." *Aujourd'hui: Arts et Architecture* vol. 10, no.57/58 (October), pp.147-153.
"Musee de Berlin-Tiergarten 1965. Trois Projets de Concourse." *Aujourd'hui: Arts et Architecture* vol.10, no.57/58 (October),

pp.141-143.
"Oswald Mathias Ungers.: (Projects) *Aujourd'hui: Arts et Architecture* vol.10, no.57/58 (October), pp.114-119.
"Quartier du Marksiches Viertel Berlin." *Aujourd'hui: Arts et Architecture* vol.10, no.57/58 (October), pp.86-101.
Ungers, O.M. "Grossform." *Aujourd'hui: Arts et Architecture* vol.10, no.57/58 (October), pp.108-113.
_____. "Form in der Grossstadt (Ruhwaldpark)." *Werk* vol.54, no.11 (November), pp.735-743.
"Architektur: Brutalismus—Rauh und Rissig." *Der Spiegel* vol.21, no.47 (13 November), pp.188-193.
"Berlin, Markisches Viertel, ein Zwischenbericht." *Bauwelt* vol.58, no.46/47 (20 November), p.1189.

1968
"Berlin—Markisches Viertel." *DLW—Nachrichten* vol.32, no.46, pp.33-50.
Feuerstein, Gunther. *New Directions in German Architecture* (New York: George Braziller), pp.33,37-38.
Hoffmann, Gretl. *Reisefuhrer zur Modernen Architektur Deutschland* (Stuttgart: Julius Hoffmann Verlag), pp.51,61, 62,63.
Ungers, O.M. (critic) "Verkehrsband Spree." *Veroffentlichungen zur Architektur* no.12 (Berlin: T.U. Berlin, March).
_____. "Die Wuppertaler Schwabebahn." *Veroffentlichungen zur Architektur* no.16 (Berlin: T.U. Berlin, July).
"O.M. Ungers: Ruppenhorn." *Deutsche Bauzeitung* vol.73, no.102 (August), pp.586-587.
Ungers, O.M. (critic). "Entwurfe fur Eine Gesamtoberschule." *Veroffentlichungen zur Architektur* no.15 (Berlin: T.U. Berlin, September).
_____. (critic) "Wohnungssysteme in Stahl." *Veroffentlichungen zur Architektur* no.17 (Berlin: T.U. Berlin, September).
_____. (critic). "Ithaca N.Y." *Veroffentlichungen zur Architektur* no.18 (Berlin: T.U. Berlin, October).
_____. (critic). "Wohnbebauungen. Stadtebauliche Ubungen 1967/1968." *Veroffentlichungen zur Architektur* no.19 (Berlin: T.U. Berlin, November).
_____. (critic) "Schnellbahn und Gegaude." *Veroffentlichungen zur Architektur* no.21 (Berlin: T.U. Berlin, December).
_____. (critic) "Wohnungssysteme in Grosstafeln." *Veroffentlichungen zur Architektur* no.22 (Berlin: T.U. Berlin, December).

1969
Albach, Horst, and O.M. Ungers. *Optimale Wohngebietsplanung* vol.1 (Wiesbaden: Betriebswirtschaftlicher Verlag Gabler).
"Wettbewerbe Projekt Flughafen Berlin-Tegel." *Lotus* 6, pp.220-229.
"Wohnungsbau in Deutschland: Gesellschaft—Esbrockelt." *Der Spiegel* vol.23, no.6 (February), pp.38-63.
Ungers, O.M. "Systemes Cellules d'Habitations." *L'Architecture d'Aujourd'hui* vol.40, no.147 (April/May), pp.71-76.
_____. (critic) "Wohnungssysteme in Raumzelle." *Veroffentlichungen zur Architektur* no.24 (Berlin: T.U. Berlin, June).
_____. "Berlin 1995." *Veroffentlichungen zur Architektur* no.25, (Berlin: T.U. Berlin, June).
_____. (critic) "Blocksanierung und Parken." *Veroffentlichungen zur Architektur* no.26 (Berlin: T.U. Berlin, June).
_____. "Berliner Brandwande." *Veroffentlichungen zur Architektur* no.27 (Berlin: T.U. Berlin, June).
Ungers, O.M. and Associates. *Modular Box Housing System—Study for Alcoa* (Ithaca, New York: O.M. Ungers, July).
"In Search of Ithaca—Cornell Students' Projects." *Architectonoki and Plastic Arts* vol.13, no.74 (July/August), pp.52-57.
Gieselmann, Reinhard and O.M. Ungers. "Towards a New Architecture (1960)." In Conrad, Ulrich, ed. *Programmes and Manifestoes on 20th Century Architecture* (Cambridge, Mass.: MIT Press), pp.165-166. Translation of "Zu einer neuen Architektur." Originally published in *Der Monat* vol.15, no.174 (March 1963), p.96.

1970
Ne Stein Vun Kolle (Koln-Braunsfeld: Verlagsgesellschaft Rudolf Muller), unpaged.
Pehnt, Wolfgang. *German Architecture 1960-1970* (New York: Praeger Publishers), pp.30,33,56,86,87-90,223.
Der Spiegel, ed. "Ausbildung der Architekten." *Mit Dem Latein Am Ende* (Hamburg: Spiegle-Verlag Rudolf Augstein KG), pp.127-134.
Ungers, O.M. (Address on architectural education), in *Ministry of Housing and Development: The Interaction of Tradition and Technology—Report of the Proceedings of the First International Congress of Architects.* (Isfahn Iran: Ministry of Housing and Development), pp.223-231.
Ungers, O.M., and Tilman Heyde. *Lysander New City (A project of Fourth and Fifth Year Students)*. (Ithaca, New York: Cornell University Department of Architecture).
Rumpf, Peter. "Kein Offentliches Schlachtfest—der BDA mit Gasten auf der Godesburg." *Bauwelt* vol.70, no.1 (5 January), pp.7-8.
Pehnt, Wolfgang. "Bauen im Deutschland der 60er Jahre." *Deutsche Bauzeitung* vol.104, no.2 (February), pp.88-103, 106-113.
Ungers, Liselotte, and Mathias, O. "Utopische Kommune in Amerika 1800-1900: Die Hutterschen Bruder." *Werk* vol.58, no.6 (June), pp.417-420.
_____. "Utopische Kommune in Amerika: Die Amana-Community." *Werk* vol.57, no.8 (August), pp.543-546.
"Umfrage zur Architektenausbildung." *Werk* vol.57, no.10 (October), pp.675-694.
Ungers, Liselotte, and Mathias, O. "Nordwest-Zentrum: Adhoc Heart of a City?" *Architectural Forum* vol.133, no.3 (October), pp.30-37.
_____. "Utopische Kommunen in America (1800-1900)." *Baumeister* vol.67, no.10 (October), pp.1167-1170.

1971
Peters, Paulhans. *Hausgruppen—Mehrfamilienhauser* (Munich: Verlag Georg DW Callwey), pp.20-22. Spanish edition: *Casas En Grupo—Viviendas Plurifamiliares* (Barcelona: Editorial Gustave Gili, S.A., 1972).
Vietorisz, Thomas (Principal Investigator). *The Design and Evaluation of Alternative Patterns of New Town Development for the State of New York* Final Report. NYS-UDC Contract no. D-49492 (Ithaca, New York: Center for Urban Development Research).
Ungers, Liselotte, and Mathias, O. "Utopische Kommune in Amerika 1800-1900: Die Owenites in New Harmony (Indiana)."

Werk vol.58, no.3 (March), pp.205-208.
Ungers, O.M. "Stadtprobleme in der pluralistichen Messengesellschaft." *Transparent* vol.2, no.5, pp.3-19.
Ungers, Liselotte, and Mathias, O. "Utopische Kommune in Amerika 1800-1900: Fourishe Phalanxen in Amerika." *Werk* vol.58, no.8 (August), pp.272-276.
_____. "Neue Kommunen in den USA—Tendenzen und Trends." *Werk* vol.58, no.9 (September), pp.627-631.
"Markisches Viertel, Berlin—Dokumentation II." *Bauwelt* vol.62, no.47/48 (29 November), pp.1914-1941.

1972
Aloi, Giampiero. *Casa de Abitazione* (2a serie) (Milano: Ulrico Hoepli Editore), pp.91-96.
Sharp, Dennis. *A Visual History of Twentieth-Century Architecture* (Greenwich, Connecticut: New York Graphic Society), pp.230-231.
Sting, Hellmuth. *Der Grundiss Im Mehrgeschossigen Wohnungsbau* (Stuttgart: Verlagsanstalt Alexander Koch GmbH), pp.20-22, 44. Spanish edition: *Plantas de Blocques de Vivienda* (Barcelona: Editorial Gustavo Gili, S.A., 1973).
Ungers, Liselotte, and Mathias, O. *Kommunen in der Neuen Welt, 1740-1970* (Cologne: Kiepenhauser und Witsch). Spanish edition: *Comunas en el Nuevo Mundo: 1740-1971* (Barcelona: Editorial Gustavo Gili, S.A., 1978).
Ungers, O.M., and Brown-Manrique, Gerardo. *S-SHHS: Self-help Housing System* (Ithaca, New York: Cornell University Department of Architecture).
"Markisches Viertel; enquete aupres des architectes." *L'Architecture d'Aujourd'hui* vol.161, no.4, (April), pp.12-15. Excerpted from *Bauwelt* vol.62, no.47/48 (29 November 1971).
Ungers, O.M.; Heyde, Tilman; and Dimock, Tom. "Eine Serie von Interaktive Planningsprogrammen—SIPP." *Werk* vol.59, no.6 (June), pp.347-352.
Muller-Romback, W. "Bauten des Bundes ind ihre Intergation in die Stadt Bonn." *Baumeister* vol.69, no.7 July, pp.755-771.
Ungers, Liselotte, and Mathias, O. "Early Communes in the USA." *Architectural Design* vol.42, no.8 (August), pp.502-512.

1973
Bonfanti, Ezio; Rosaldo Bonicalzi; Aldo Rossi; Massimo Scolari; and Daniele Vitale. *Architettura Razionale* (Milano: Franco Agneli Editore), pp.90,91,250-252.
Dielmann, Harald; Jorg C. Kirschenmann; and Herbert Pfeiffer. *Wohnungsbau—The Dwelling—L'Habitat* (Stuttgart: Karl Kramer Verlag), pp.36,52,53,139,154. Spanish edition: *El Habitat* (Barcelona: Editorial Gustavo Gili, S.A., 1974).
Schalhorn, Konrad. "Wohungen fur Alte Menschen" *Entwruf und Planung* no.17 (Munich: Verlag George DW Callway), pp.50-51, 69.
Schmalscheidt, Hans. "Studentenheime" *Entwurf and Planung* no.21 (Munich: Verlag George DW Callwey), pp.31,32,96-97, 119,122-123.

1974
Ungers, Liselotte and O. Mathias. "Le Comuni del Nuovo Mondo." *Lotus* 8, pp.92-95.
Ungers, O.M. (Comments on housing), in Smithson, Alison, ed. *Team 10 Primer*. Revised edition. (Cambridge, Massachusetts: MIT Press), p.18.
_____. "A Subjective Study of the LA freeway Grid." *On Site* 5/6, pp.52-56.
"Zwischen Tiergarten und Landwehrkanal." *Bauwelt* vol.65, no.19 (20 May), pp.714-719.

1975
Nevins, Deborah, ed. *The Roosevelt Island Housing Competition*. Exhibition catalogue. (New York: Wittenborn Art Books, Inc.), unpaged, entry no.34.
Ungers, O.M. "The Hofe." *Lotus* 10, pp.160-161.
_____. "Projekte als Typologische Collagen." in Keliheus, Josef Paul, ed. "Das Prinzip Reihung in Der Architektur." *Dortmunder Architekturhefte* no.2, pp.169-171.
Ungers, O.M. and Dietszch, K.L. "Eine Entscheidung." *Bauwelt* vol.66, no.20/21 (30 May), pp.612-613.
Colquhoun, Alan. "Rational Architecture." *Architectural Design* vol.45, no.6 (June), pp.365-370.
Stadtebaulicher Ideenwettbewerb Berlin-Lichterfelde 4. Ring." *Wettbewerbe Aktuell* no.6 (June), cover, pp.361-372.
Bode, Peter M. "Potembin Wusste es besser." *Der Spiegel* vol.29, no.44 (27 October), pp.228-232.
"Homage to Olmstead and Others." *Architectural Record* vol.158, no.10 (October), p.116.
Aymonino, Carlo. "Il contributo di Oswald Mathias Ungers all'Architettura." *Controspazio* vol.7, no.3 (November), pp.2-43.
"Rationale Architektur." *Prolegomena* 15, Vienna: vol.4, no.4 (November), pp.38-42.
Agrest, Diana and Latour, Alessandra. "Sviluppo urbano e forma della citta a New York." *Controspazio* vol.7, no.4 (December).

1976
Banham Reyner. *Megastructure—Urban Futures of the Recent Past* (New York: Harper & Row), pp.158-159.
"Berlin Alt und New——Zur Integration moderner Architektur in Altbaustrukturen." IDZ-Berlin (International Design Center, Berlin): *IDZ-Berlin Jahresbericht '75* (Berlin: International Design Zentrum).
Gregotti, Vittorio. "Oswald Mathias Ungers." *Lotus 11*, p.12.
Kleihues, Josef Paul, ed. "Dortmunder Architekturausstellung 1976." *Dortmunder Architekturhefte* no.3, unpaged.
Nestler, Paolo and Peter M. Bode. *Deutsche Kunst Seit 1960— Architektur* (Munich: Verlag F. Bruckmann KG), p.39.
Schneider, Martina, ed. *Entwerfen in der Historischen Strasse (Werstadt 3)* (Berlin: Abakon Verlagsgessellschaft), pp.82-97.
_____. "Note—Berlin-Alt und Neu." *Lotus* 13, pp.25-26.
Ungers, O.M. "Designing and Thinking in Images, Metaphors and Analogies." *MANtransForms* Exhibition catalogue. (New York: Cooper-Hewitt Museum, Smithsonian Institution), pp.98-113.
_____. "Morphological Exercises." *Lotus* 13, pp.48-55.
_____. "Planning Criteria." *Lotus* 11, p.13.
_____. Projects. *Lotus* 11, pp.14-41.
_____. *Stadtebauliche Studie fur den Bereich Zwischen Schlosspark und Musuempark in Braunschweig* (Cologne: O.M. Ungers).
_____. *Vorschlag fur Die Bebauung Des Grundstucks An Der Ritterstrasse In Marburg* (Cologne: O.M. Ungers).
Ungers, O.M.; Gohner, Werner; Ovaska, Arthur; and Kollhoff, Hans.

The Urban Block and Gotham City—Metaphors and Metamorphosis—Two Concurrent Projects (Ithaca, New York: College of Architecture, Art and Planning, Cornell University).
Brown-Manrique, Gerardo. "Two Housing Programs: A Comparison of the NYS-UDC and the INFONAVIT." *Le Carre Bleu* no.2, pp.7-21.
Mamoli, Marcello. "La citta Tedesca e la formazione del Quadro urbano nella Republica Federale." *Parametro* no.48, (July/August), pp.20-39.
Blake, Peter. "Fun and Dazzle Rivaling Dadaism of the Twenties." *Smithsonian* vol.7, no.8 (November), pp.72-76.

1977

Carlini, Alessandro and Berhard Schneider. "El adoyer fur die Wiedereinfuhrung der Salle—eine Ausstellung zum Semiotischen Kolloquium, Berlin 1975." In Posner, Roland and Reinecke, Hans-Peter, eds. *Zweichenprozesse—Semiotische Forschung In Den Einzelwissenschaften* (Weisbaden: Akademische Verlaggsgesellschaft Athenaiom).
Engel, H.; Weber, K.; Duttmann, W.; Heinrichs, G.; Kleihues, J.P.; Muller, H. Ch.; Sawade, J.; and Ungers, O.M. *1776-1976 200 Jahre Berlin* (Cologne: Studioverlag fur Architektur L. Ungers).
Grafica 80—Architettura Exhibition catalogue. (Milan: Galeria di via Langone).
Klotz, Heinrich. *Architekktur in Der Bundesrepublik—Gesprache Mit Gunter Behnisch, Wolfgang Doring, Helmut Hentrick, Hans Kammerer, Frei Otto, Oswald Mathias Ungers* (Marburg: Ullstein), pp.263-316.
Kultermann, Udo. *Die Architektur IM 20.* (Cologne: Dumont Buchverlag), pp.127, 155, 158.
Logan, Donn. "Housing and Urbanism." In Davis, Same, ed. *The Form of Housing* (New York: Van Nostrand Reinhold), pp.41-63.
Mackay, David. *Multiple Family Housing—From Aggregation to Integration* (New York: Architectural Book Publishing Co.), pp.146-151.
Ungers, O.M. *Braunschweiger Morphologie* Exhibition catalogue. (Braunschweig Vermessungsant). *Die Stadt in Der Stadt—Berlin Das Grune Stadtarchipel* (Cologne: Studioverlag fur Architektur L. Ungers).
Ungers, O.M.; Kollhoff, H.F.; and Ovaska, A.A., *The Urban Villa—A Multi Family Dwelling Type* (Cologne: Studioverlag fur Architektur L. Ungers).
_____. "Project for Braunschweig Castle Park." *Lotus* 14 (March), pp.100-127.
_____. "Project for Morsbroich Castle Museum in Leverkusen." *Lotus* 14 (March), pp.98-99.
Weydemann, Thomas and Rohl, Kirsten. "Biennale Venedig 1976." *Bauwelt* vol.68, no.2 (14 January), pp.72-73.
_____. "Ideen zur Stadtgestalt (IDZ-Symposium Landwehrkanal Berlin)." *Bauwelt* vol.68, no.2 (14 January), pp.70-71.
"Architekten: Kistenmacher im Busserheind." *Der Spiegel* vol.31, no.39 (19 September), pp.206-223.
Klotz, Heinrich. "Alstadtische Moderne—Marburg versuch zur Integration von Alt und Neu." *Der Zeit* (21 October). Reprinted in: Klotz, Heinrich. *Gestaltung Einer Neuen Umwelt—Kritische Essays Zur Architektur Der Gegenwart* (Luzern: Verlag C.J. Bucher, 1978).
Ungers, O.M. (Projects.) *Space Design* no.157 (Tokyo, October), pp.25-38.
Peters, Paulhans. "Lucken busser? Erganzungen? Aussagen? Zum Bauen in alten Stadten." *Baumeister* vol.74, no.12 (December), p.1116.
Ungers, O.M. "Entwerfen mit Vorstellungsbildern, Methaphern und Analogien." *Bauwelt* vol.68, no.47/48 (23 December), pp.312-317. *(Stadtbauwelt* 56, pp.1650-1655).
"A View of Contemporary World Architecture." *Architecture and Urbanism (A + U)* no.12 (December), p.151.
"27 Architekturstudenten von Karlsplatz." *Prolegomena Vienna* vol.6, no.4 (December).

1978

Jencks, Charles. *The Language of Postmodern Architecture.* Revised edition. (New York: Rizzoli International).
Klotz, Heinrich. *Gestaltung Einer Neuen Emwelt—Kritische Essays Zur Architektur Der Gegenwart* (Luzern: Verlag C.J. Bucher).
Koolhaas, Rem. *Delirious New York—A Retroactive Manifesto for Manhattan* (New York: Oxford University Press). London: Thames & Hudson Ltd.).
Brown-Manrique, Gerardo. "Two Housing Programs: A Comparison of the NYS-UDC and the INFONAVIT." *Le Carre Bleu* no.2, pp.7-21.
Mamoli, Marcello. "La citta Tedesca e la formazione del Quadro urbano nella Republica Federale." *Parametro* no.48, (July/August), pp.20-39.
Blake, Peter. "Fun and Dazzle Rivaling Dadaism of the Twenties." *Smithsonian* vol.7, no.8 (November), pp.72-76.
Raggi, Franco, ed. *Europa/America—Architecture Urbane Alternative Suburbane* (Venice: Edizioni la Biennale di Venezia), pp.78-85.
Rational Architecture Rationnelle 1978—La Reconstruction de la Ville Europeene/The Reconstruction of the European City (Brussels: Editions des Archives d'Architecture Moderne), pp.70-72, 102-103, 122-124, 127.
Sharp, Dennis, ed. *The Rationalists—Theory and Design in the Modern Movement* (London: The Architectural Press), pp.211-212.
Stadt Marburg. Neues Bauten in Del Alten Stadt—Ausstellung Zu Projekten Fur Die Marburg Alstadt (Marburg: Druckerei Wenzel).
Ungers, O.M., and Borchers, G. "Plannungsbeispiel Siedlung, Hochlamark Rechinhausen." *Dortmunder Architekturhefte* no.11.
Ungers, O.M.; Koolhaas, Rem; Riemann, Peter; Koolhoff, Hans; and Ovaska, Arthur. "Cities Within the City—Proposals by the Sommer Akademie for Berlin" *Lotus* 19, pp.82-97.
Jencks, Charles. "Late Modernism and Post-Modernism." *Architectural Design* vol.48, no.11-12 (November/December), pp.592-609.
Klotz, Heinrich. "Auf dem einsamen Weg von De Cirico—Platz zur Treppe ins Nichts" *Bauwelt* vol.69, no.1 (6 January), pp.26-29.
"Cornell Team Selected for West Berlin Hotel" *American Institute of Architects Journal* vol.67, no.2 (February), pp.22, 78.
Kuhvert, Nikolaus, and Reiss-Schmidt, Stephan. "Thesen sur 'Rationalen Architektur—Entwerfen mit Invarianzen und Vorstellungsbilden." *Arch+* no.37 (April), pp.28-38.
"Wettbewerb Hotel Berlin, Berlin" *Bauen Und Wohnen* no.4 (April), pp.173-176.
Schumacher, Thomas. "James Stirling and O.M. Ungers: Five Museum Projects" *Skyline* no.1 (1 April), p.3.

Bode, Peter M. "Die Neuen Museen." *Westermanns Monatschefte* no.4 (April), pp.44-53.
Kleihues, J.P. "Empfehlungen und Vorschlage fur 5 Wohnsiedlungen im Revier." *Bauwelt* vol.69, no.14 (14 April), pp.552-553.
Ungers, O.M. "Siedlung Hochlarmark, Rechlinghausen." *Bauwelt* vol.69, no.14 (14 April), pp.562-563.
??????. "The Vienna Superblocks." *Oppositions* no.13, (Summer), p.83.
"Kumpel Antons Hauschen und die Dortmunder Architekturtage." *Baumeister* vol.75, no.6 (June), p.485.
Lang, George Willibald, and Horst, Peter Richter. "Stadterneuerung zwischen Architekturasthetik und Politish verantwortlicher Planung." *Bauwelt* vol.69, no.25 (7 July), pp.991-996.
Dischkoff, Nikola, and Wilkens, Michael. "Stadtplanunh: ein fach Konzepte gewohnlich. *Baumeister* vol.75, no.8 (August), pp.687-694.
Ungers, O.M. "Das Stadthaus—The Urban Villa." *Dai—Zeitschrift* vol.18 (August/September), pp.55-56.
"Internationale Bauausstellung 1984." *Berliner Baubilanz 1978* (Berlin: Senator fur Bau- und Wohnungswessen, September), pp.56+.
Hoffmann-Axthelm, Dieter. "Vom Ungang mit zerstorter Stadtgeschichte—festgemachtam Berliner Ausstellungsobjekt sudliche Friedrichstadt." *Arch+* no.40-41 (November), pp.14-22.
Pesch, Franz, and Klaus, Selle. "'Rationale Architektur' im Revier—ein Nachwort zu den 4." *Dortmunder Architekturtagen. Arch+* no.42 (December), pp.44-50.
Peters, Paul Hans. "Die Letzen 20 Jahre in der Architektur/The Last Twenty Years in Architecture." *Baumeister* vol.75, no.12 (December).

1979
The Best in Exhibition Designs." *Print Casebook 3—1978/1979 Edition* (Washington, D.C.: R.C. Publications, Inc.), pp.31-34.
Geiselmann, Reinhard. *Wohnbau* (Braunschweig/Wiesbaden: Friedrich Vieweg u. Sohn), pp.23, 92, 100.
Kleihues, J.P., ed. "Museumsbauten—Entwurfe und Projekte Seit 1945." *Dortmunder Architekturhefte* no.15.
Ungers, O.M. *Kommentar Zum Wettbewerb Kammergericht Berlin* (Cologne: Studioverlag fur Architektur L. Ungers).
??????. "Pyramus and Thisbe—Two Small Houses in Berlin." *Lotus* 22, pp.18-19.
Ungers, O.M.; Killhoff, Hans F.; and Ovaska, Arthur A. *The Urban Garden—Student Projects for the Sudliche Friedrichstadt Berlin* (Cologne: Studioverlag fur Architektur L. Ungers).
Ungers, O.M. "Architektur der Erinnerrung." *Der Architekt* no.1 (January), pp.43-47.
??????. "Fur eine visionare Architektur der Erinnerung—Pour une architecture visionnaire du souvenir." *Werk-Archithese* vol.66, no.25/26 (January/February), pp.4-6.
"Die Moderne ist tot—et lebe die Post Moderne; wir Drauchen keine Neue Utopien, sondem Erinnergung?" *Die Welt* (20 February).
Hollein, Hans. "Hans Hollein und die Ausstellung MAN-transFORMS." *Deutsche Bauzeitung* no.3 (March), pp.35-41.
"Stadtebaulicher Ideenwettbewerb Kammergericht Berlin." *Wettbewerbe Arkuell* no.4 (April), pp.241-256.
"O.M. Ungers. Architektur in Deutschland." *Das Kunstwerk* vol.32, no.2/3, (April/June), pp.132-141.
??????. "Kommentar zu einer humanistischen Architektur." *Das Kunstwerk* vol.32, no.2/3 (April/June), pp.133-141.
"Visionen des Oswald Mathias Ungers." *Werk-Archithese* vol.66, no.29/30 (May/June), p.73.
Kultermann, Udo. "Ein Haus muss seine wurzeln in der Geschichte haben." *Die Welt* no.144, (23 June).
Peters, Paulhaus. "Kommentar: Internationale Bauausstellung 1984' Berlin." *Baumeister* vol.76, no.6 (June 1979), pp.560-562.
"Stadtebaulicher Ideenwettbewerb Kammergericht Berlin—Programmatisch." *Bauwelt* vol.70, no.26 (13 July), p.1104.
Klotz, Heinrich. "Der Fall Oswald Mathias Ungers." *Deutsche Bauzeitung* no.10 (October), pp.15-18.
Ungers, O.M. *Deutsche Bauzeitung* no.10 (October), pp.19-24.
Blomeyer, Gerald. "Supreme Court Competition, West Berlin." *International Architect* vol.1, no.1, p.9.
Maxwell, Robert. "Charles Jencks and 'The Evolution From Modern Architecture'," *International Architect* vol.1, no.1, pp.10-11.
Peckham, Andrew. "Rational Architecture: European Style versus British." *International Architect* vol.1, no.1, pp.64-65.
Ungers, O.M. "Urban Intervention: Supreme Court Design for West Berlin 1979." *International Architect* vol.1, no.2, pp.47-60.
Bofinger, H.; Klotz, M.H.; and Pahe, J., eds. *Architektur In Dertschland* (Stuttgart: Verlag W. Kohlhammer GmbH, 1979), pp.171-179.
Joedecke, Jurgen. *Architektur Im Umbrunch* (Stuttgart: ArchPaper-Edition Kramer, 1979), pp.201, 202, 219, 221.
Senator fur Bau-und Wohnungswesen: 5 Architektuen Zeichen Fur Berlin (Berlin: Archibook Verlag, 1979), pp.28-33, 96-113.
Ungers, O.M. "Architecture of the Collective Memory (The Infinite Catalogue of Urban Form)." *Lotus* 24 (1979), pp.5-11.
Bofinger, Helge. "Nowhere Man Sitting in his Nowhere Land...." *Der Arhcitekt* no.7/8 (July/August), pp.363-365.
Ungers, O.M. "Komplement: Pyramus und Thisbe an Spandaus Stadtmauern—ein momentum moriam—oder fur Berlin geplant und nicht Gebaut." *Neue Heimat Monatshefte* no.8 (August), pp.56-57.
Coersmeier, Urich. "Leistungsbild im Bauwettbewerb." *Der Architekt* no.9 (September), pp.401-403.
Kloz, Heirich. "Uber Vorentwurfe—ohne anspruch fertiger Antworten—zum Gesprach das Burgerschaft." *Neue Heimat Monatshefte* no.9 (September), pp.14-23.
Ungers, O.M. "Humanistische Architektur." *Deutsches Architektenblatt* vol.11, no.9 (1 September), pp.1025-1028.
Holl, Steven. "Ungers at Columbia." *Skyline* vol.2, no.5 (October), p.14.
Ungers, Liselotte and Mathias, O. "Mauern konnen auch die Spekulanten unser ruf ergemt zum Bauen." *'DU'—Die Kunstzeitschrift* no.10 (October), pp.36-39, 81.
Breitling, Peter. "Die Architektur der Besserwisser." *Baumeister* vol.76, no.12 (December), pp.1225-1234.
Assonometria Exhibition Catalogue. (Milan: Franco Agneli Editore, 14 December).
"Hotel und Gestaltung Budapester-/Kurfurstenstrasse, Berlin." *Architektur Wettbewerbe* no.12 (December), p.63.
van Eyck, Aldo. "Un Messagio a Mathias Ungers da un atro mundo." *Spazio E Societa* vol.2, no.8 (December), pp.63-64.

1980

"City Segments." *Design Quarterly* 113/114 (Minneapolis: Walker Art Center), pp.78-79.

Vogt, Adolf Max. *Architektur 1940-1980* (Frankfurt am Main: Propylaen Verlag Ullstein GmbH), pp.111, 176, 202, 204, 256-257.

Ungers, O.M. (in conversation with Marcello Panzarella). "Una teoria transformatione Morfologiche." *Architettura—Giornale Della Progettazione* (January/February), p.3.

"Construire la rue: Projet de Cour d'Appel a Berlin, Projet d'Immeuble, Berlin. *L'Architecture d'Aujourd'hui* no.207 (February), pp.38-42.

"Ungers—Plane fur das Schloss Morsbroich Leverkusen." *Bauwelt* vol.71, no.9 (February), pp.306-307.

Watson, Eric. "The Case of O.M. Ungers." *Skyline* vol.2, no.7 (February), p.11.

"Badische Landesbibliotek, Karlsruhe." *Architektur Und Wettbewerbe* no.101 (March), cover, pp.29-33.

Berni, Lorenzo. "Progetto per la Corte d'Appelo di Berlin." *Panorama* (31 March), p.45.

"Badische Landesbibliothek Karlsruhe." *Wettbewerbe Artuell* no.5 (May), pp.279-292.

Lampugnani, Vittorio Magnano. "Architektur als ein stuck—Neuen Tendenzes des Bauens—zum Wettbewerb fur die Landesbibliothek in Karlsruhe." *Frankfurter Allgemeine Zeitung* no.92 (19 April), p.25.

"Wettbewerb Landesbibliothek Karlsruhe." *Bauwelt* vol.71, no.14 (11 April), pp.578-584.

Project Collaborators

Hotel Berlin
Hans Kollhoff, Thomas Will

Architecture Museum
K.L. Dietzsch, Barbara Taha

Perimeter Block, Schillerstrasse
Irene Keil, Jürgen Leitner, Bernd Wippler

Carlsburg Hochschule
K.L. Dietzsch, Burkhard Meyer, Barbara Taha

Baden State Library
K.L. Dietzsch, Burkhard Meyer, Geoffrey Wooding

Ideas Competition
Lazlo Kiss, Simon Ungers, Geoffrey Wooding

Lützowplatz
K.L. Dietzsch, Burkhard Meyer, Bernd Wippler

Hildesheim
Irene Keil, Jürgen Leitner

Konstantinplatz
Irene Keil, Jürgen Leitner, Burkhard Meyer